ACKNOWLEDGMENTS

If some things in life take a village, writing a book such as this requires a small township. Without a doubt, the honorary mayor of my little town is IGFA Librarian Gail Morchower. Without her inexhaustible good humor, encyclopedic brain, and meticulous fact-checking, this book would have been much more painful to write and much less pleasant to read. Even more difficult is overstating her everyday contributions to the IGFA, an organization she so ably and loyally represents. Thus, here's a sweeping bow to you, Gail. A mere tip of the cap is not nearly enough.

Many other townfolk must be recognized as well. To sitting IGFA President Rob Kramer, a heartfelt thank-you for seeing the potential of this project and allowing it go forward. To IGFA Past President Mike Leech for the fishing, the lunches, and the insights. You still owe me a swordfish. To IGFA staffers Lesley Arico, Adrian Gray, Glenda Kelley, Linda Irwin, Mike Myatt, Jason Schratwieser, Lynda Wilson and others who gave generously of their time and encouragement. To angling pioneers John W. (Jack) Anderson, Alfred C. Glassell, Jr., Peter Goadby, George Matthews, and Mark Sosin, all of whom were most patient with my pedantic questioning. Finally, to my long-time amigo, IGFA Trustee and fellow Tuna Club member Mike Farrior. Nice to have you up and around again, old buddy, and thanks once again for all that you've done and will continue to do.

TABLE OF CONTENTS

FOREWORD

The history of IGFA is almost like the history of angling itself. Although ancient anglers were hooking fish shortly after the dawn of history, it was not until the 1930s that big-game fishing started to come into its own. Writers like Ernest Hemingway, Zane Grey and Kip Farrington popularized offshore angling for great fish and captured the imagination of millions of readers around the world. It was in this era, in 1939, that IGFA was founded to verify and chronicle the great catches of the world. In order to do this, a universal set of ethical angling rules had to be established. More than six-and-a-half decades later the IGFA rules stand strong as the measure by which all world records are judged.

Mike Rivkin, the author of this book, took the project on as a labor of love. Making many trips from his native California to the E. K. Harry Library of Fishes at IGFA headquarters, Rivkin pored over countless files, historic documents, club newsletters and personal correspondence. Many interviews took place with people who helped shape modern-day IGFA. Thousands of historic photos from the archives were reviewed, resulting in this lavishly-illustrated account.

This book is not a dry chronology of IGFA events. Rivkin has given these pages life with anecdotes pulled from IGFA files. He brings us from the beginnings of the organization in New York's American Museum of Natural History to the international organization of today, housed in a multi-million dollar, 60,000-square-foot facility, with members and representatives in far corners of the globe.

From the early beginnings with Michael Lerner, followed by the eras of IGFA Presidents Bill Carpenter, E. K. Harry, Mike Leech and Rob Kramer, this book covers the fishing events, people and records of the past 66 years.

We warmly thank Mike Rivkin for creating *Big-Game Fishing Headquarters: A History of the IGFA*. Without his vision and commitment, this important part of angling history would never have appeared as such a fascinating book.

George G. Matthews
IGFA Chairman

PREFACE

First, there is a self-evident truth. In the relative importance of great historical events, the history of the IGFA would probably rank somewhere below the Battle of Gettysburg and the Human Genome Project. There is no scholarly paper trail a mile wide, no hallowed hall full of academics quick to haggle over every point, and no sweeping change-the-world conclusions to extract. However, that doesn't make it any less interesting. Indeed, few organizations have legacies as rich and enduring as the IGFA. Its 66-year (and counting) lifespan includes fascinating personalities, spirited controversy, great stories of adventure, and the triumph of good sportsmanship and conservation over wasteful excess. That angling is a spiritual pursuit for countless practitioners adds something to the yarn as well. In short, the history of the IGFA is a rollicking good story long overdue in the telling.

As with most things, organizations have their own biases and so do authors. Despite the fact that the IGFA today encompasses angling in all types of water, it was most definitely a saltwater fishing organization for the first 39 years of its life. More precisely, the IGFA's early emphasis was almost exclusively on big-game fishing for tuna and billfish, often in distant waters. The organization's founder, early officers, and all of its long-time Presidents utilized heavy tackle in pursuit of these largest of game fish. Not until 1978 did the IGFA even glance in the direction of freshwater anglers, but it has since compiled an increasingly credible record in reaching out to that constituency. Nevertheless, the focus of the IGFA has traditionally been towards the big-game angler, and so it is of this book.

If there is any exception to the above, it is the IGFA's long-time institutional contempt for sharks. Despite their size and fearsome reputation, most sharks have little fighting ability and can often be taken in great size with relatively little effort. In fairness, there are a few notable exceptions — mako and thresher sharks are both world-class fighters — but sharks as a class are generally not thought of as sporting fish. For many years, the IGFA even classified shark records separately due to their cartilaginous (i.e., non-bony) nature, but this was really just an excuse for turning them into a second-class quarry. Nonetheless, shark fishing does not play a prominent role in the IGFA history, and the avid shark angler looking for news of his sport will find little of interest here.

Shark fishing did have one prominent adherent in the early days of big-game angling, and that was Zane Grey. Grey tangled with many sharks during his pioneering expeditions in the 1920s and '30s, and his books unabashedly praise their sporting qualities. In this and other areas, and despite his prodigious angling accomplishments, Grey spent most of his career at odds with the angling mainstream. He always fished by himself or with his brother R.C., he never competed in tournaments, and he died the year the IGFA was founded. Indeed, it appears that he never fished with Michael Lerner or any of the other early IGFA principals. As a result, notwithstanding his enormously important role as a pioneering angler and promoter of the sport, he is not a large part of the IGFA story.

Also worthy of comment at this juncture is the matter of references. The lack of a comprehensive bibliography at the conclusion of this book is not meant to discourage scholarship. Rather, it should be viewed as an invitation to patronize the E.K. Harry Library of Fishes at the IGFA Fishing Hall of Fame in Dania Beach, Florida. Aside from the personal interviews, all of the references are there: the agendas, albums, articles, artifacts, books, brochures, files, letters, manuscripts, minutes, newspapers, photographs, records, souvenirs, transcripts, videos and more that combine to make this story so compelling. There are a hundred books yet to be written from its many thousands of sources, and the setting is as lovely and tranquil as any library in the world. Many are the IGFA Trustees, Representatives, employees and visitors who pass through the Library and wish for months instead of minutes to fully explore its contents. The Library is open seven days a week to all comers, and it's an experience not to be missed.

Finally, a word about records. One of the most admirable things about the IGFA is its adherence to the ethical high road in evaluating world record claims. World records serve as currency in today's world: they attract sponsors, generate publicity, and even look good on resumes. Of the nearly one thousand record applications submitted each year to the IGFA, the organization must ultimately make a subjective decision on the efficacy of each one. That very few records are granted and then rescinded speaks enormously well for the rigor of the process. Nevertheless, errors are occasionally made, both in the record-granting process and in books like this one. Where there are conflicting claims as to the invention of this or the first capture of that (and there are many), I've done my best to arbitrate. While all errors and omissions are mine alone, I stand ready to learn of and correct any egregious oversights. In the meantime, enjoy the story and best wishes for smooth seas and tight lines.

Mike Rivkin
May 2005

A day's catch of albacore off Catalina Island in 1904.

Chapter One

BIG-GAME FISHING HISTORY

Few of man's recreational pursuits are such a part of recorded history as is angling. Imprints of fishing scenes can be found on ancient Egyptian tombs, and references to fishing in the writings of Aristotle, Homer, and Pliny the Elder are frequent. While even those ancient scribes were prone to piscatorial overstatement, accounts of fish behavior and characteristics set down by subsistence fishermen of the period are remarkably consistent with modern observations. Relatively little about angling was recorded during the first millennium, but the Middle Ages witnessed a resurgence in ichthyological interest as the natural world was once again in favor. The invention of the printing press also helped to bring the undersea world to a wider audience than ever before. Many printed works were ornamented with exquisite hand-colored woodcuts and engravings, and the representation of sea monsters was a particularly popular theme.

Despite often wild speculation by early naturalists, it wasn't until the scientific voyages of Baudin, Bouganville, Cook, and others that very much was known about marine science. As a result of their painstaking collection efforts in the late 18th and early 19th centuries, the first substantial ichthyological collections were formed by the major scientific institutes of London and Paris. Among the earliest ichthyologists to emerge was Swiss-born Louis Agassiz (1807-1873), a mesmerizing personality who did much to train many future naturalists during his long Harvard tenure. By that time, a small but seminal body of angling literature was in place, including Berner's *Treatyse of Fysshynge wyth an Angle* (1496), Walton's *Compleat Angler* (1653), and Richard Brookes' *The Art of Angling, Rock and Sea-Fishing* (1740). The first two works are still in print today, and Brookes' treatise bears the distinction of being the first to place emphasis on saltwater fishing.

By the mid-1800s, recreational angling with rod and reel was well underway. In England, coastal angling from rocks and piers for "coarse fish"[1] was a popular pursuit, and fly casting in both fresh and saltwater settings was gaining adherents. Across the Atlantic, anglers along America's eastern

---

[1]*Essentially everything but salmon and trout.*

14

Where big-game fishing began: Avalon Harbor on California's Santa Catalina Island (photo ca. 1940).

seaboard were catching bass, bluefish, cod, kingfish, saltwater trout,[2] and other coastal species. When one intrepid angler captured a 70 lb black drum on sporting tackle, it created quite a stir. The growing sport received another boost when American naturalist G. Brown Goode published his remarkably comprehensive *Game Fishes of the United States* in 1878. His description of game fish as "...those which, by reason of their cunning, courage, strength, beauty, and the sapidity[3] of their flesh, are sought for by those who angle for sport with delicate fishing tackle" fluttered the hearts of early sportsmen. While neither Goode nor his readers could imagine the capture of a fish larger than 100 lb in anything like a sporting manner, the discovery of giant tarpon in Florida would soon change their views.

An early catch of Florida tarpon.

One of the first saltwater species to be declared a game fish, the tarpon (*Megalops atlanticus*) probably was well known to early native Americans but relatively late in coming to the attention of science. Florida's isolation from the rest of North America surely didn't help, and the fish wasn't properly classified by science until around 1850. However, when its extensive population and range were finally identified, tarpon burst onto the angling scene as the first big-game saltwater fish worthy of serious attention. Fly fishers A.W. Dimock and his son Julian became minor celebrities in the early 1880s with their ground-breaking pursuit of tarpon on a fly, and the capture of a foul-hooked 172 lb tarpon in 1884 by S.H. Jones dispelled the notion that large fish couldn't be taken on rod and reel. The sporting press quickly became ecstatic in its embrace of tarpon fishing, and the rush that followed resulted in many of these acrobatic but inedible fish being needlessly killed. Nevertheless, a conservation ethic quickly took hold, and tarpon fishing today remains one of the cornerstones of big-game angling around the world. There are few pastimes more exciting.

15

---

[2]*Better known today as weakfish or sea trout.*
[3]*The quality of having taste and flavor.*

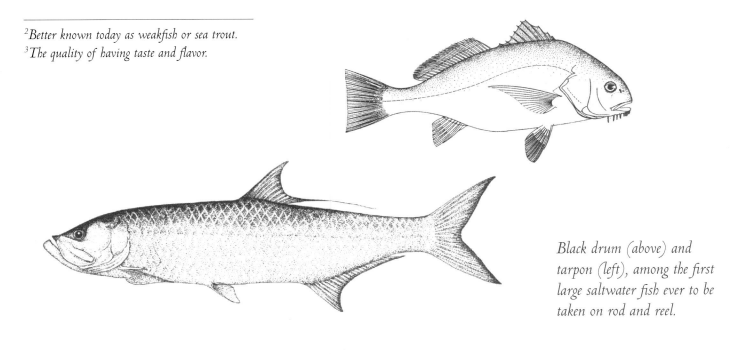

Black drum (above) and tarpon (left), among the first large saltwater fish ever to be taken on rod and reel.

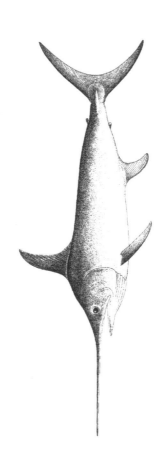

Swordfish were known to charge fishing vessels and thus were greatly feared by early mariners.

By the close of the 19th century, many other species were coming to the attention of Florida anglers. The first bonefish *(Albula spp.)* and Atlantic sailfish *(Istiophorus platypterus)* taken by sportsmen were both captured around the same time in 1893. Although many conflicting claims exist relative to sailfish, the first documented catch may have been that made by a British naval officer off the coast of East Africa in 1889. By the early 20th century, sailfish[4] were known to be abundant off Florida's east coast but not often pursued. When the Long Key Fishing Camp opened in 1907, such early angling luminaries as Van Campen Heilner and Zane Grey fished there primarily for tarpon and king mackerel. Sailfish were considered a menace and something to be avoided.

Other species of billfish were even more misunderstood. The broadbill swordfish *(Xiphias gladius)* had been noted by Aristotle and its harpooning later described by many early writers. Attacks by swordfish upon fishing vessels were often reported, sometimes in hyperbolic detail. Nevertheless, billfish science was a muddle with the generic name "swordfish" used for all billed species. Atlantic sailfish were first described in the mid-17th century, but the larger Pacific sailfish *(Istiophorus platypterus)* was not identified until a century later. Interestingly, a Pacific sailfish specimen was collected during one of Cook's voyages to the South Pacific but was subsequently overlooked for decades after his return. Adding to the confusion, a black marlin taken

---

[4] *Known as "spike fish" or "boohoo".*

by Cook near Sumatra was originally identified as a sailfish, but subsequent inspections showed it to be an entirely different species. As recently as 1940, credence was given to a wildly inaccurate report that sailfish could grow to 25' in length. Thus did gamefish ichthyology enter the 20th century with very much to learn.

Perhaps best known of all the future big-game species was the tuna. The Greek naturalist Aristotle was familiar with many tuna characteristics, including its potential to reach considerable size. Other early commentators noted the tuna's migratory habits and even their tendency to take feathered lures.[5] An active Mediterranean tuna fishery also provided many fresh examples for inspection. While no species distinction was noted until the mid-1500s, much scientific progress was made in the subsequent 150 years. By the year 1850, most species of tuna had been firmly identified.[6] Recreational trolling for small tuna from maritime vessels was already common, and larger specimens were being harpooned for their oil content.[7] Enormous examples of commercially-taken tuna piqued anglers' interest, but it was surely impossible to land a giant tuna on the crude sporting tackle of the day. Almost everyone thought so…except for Dr. Charles Frederick Holder.

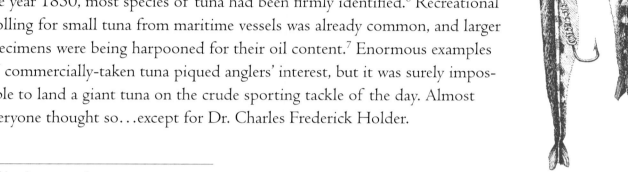

Early feather lures.

---

[5]*Although nets were the most common means of capture.*
[6]*Even the albacore (*Thunnus alalunga*) with its distinctively long pectoral fins.*
[7]*Larger fish would often yield 20 gallons of oil or more.*

A British angler trolls for mackerel in this turn-of-the-century engraving.

Dr. Charles Frederick Holder: author, naturalist, sportsman, and founder of the world's first big-game fishing club. His contributions to the sport of saltwater angling are immeasurable.

Geen's Spiral Spinner

Of all the legendary anglers that followed, none were as influential to the sport of big-game fishing as was Holder. Born in Lynn, Massachusetts in 1851, Charles Holder was the son of Emily and Dr. J.B. Holder, a family of Quakers that could trace its roots back to the time of the Pilgrims. Physician, scientist, educator, and author, the first Dr. Holder was a classic renaissance man with a breathtaking variety of interests and accomplishments. His appointment and subsequent success as Curator of Zoology at the American Museum of Natural History in New York contributed enormously to the Museum's early reputation. Beginning at age 10, young Holder often accompanied his father and Louis Agassiz on collecting trips to Florida where he developed a passionate interest in the natural world. Following a first-rate private education, Charles joined his father at the Museum to prepare for a life in science. He also discovered in himself an innate talent for writing and came to serve as the Museum's first unofficial press agent, writing hundreds of promotional articles covering all aspects of the Museum's operation. Along the way, he met and married his wife, Elizabeth Ufford, in 1879. Despite a seemingly robust constitution,[8] Holder fell seriously ill a few years later and decided to move to southern California for its forgiving climate. His 30 years there would yield a lasting legacy.

---

[8]*In his youth he was a noted boxer, wrestler, yachtsman, and even competed with broadswords.*

Already an accomplished angler by virtue of his time spent in Florida, Holder was anxious to test the waters off California to see what they might yield. Upon visiting the beautiful nearby island of Santa Catalina, he was elated to find its shoreline waters brimming with barracuda, black sea bass, bonito, yellowtail, and white sea bass. Nevertheless, he watched with dismay as locals used handlines to pull dozens of fish ashore, depositing them on the beach with little ceremony and no thought given either to sport or conservation. Holder was incensed, and it became his life's work to banish this practice in favor of one in which the fish and fisherman battled on equal terms. He led by example, personally breaking copious amounts of flimsy tackle in attempting to demonstrate that large blue water fish could be captured in a most sporting manner. When he finally did so, Charles F. Holder created the modern-day sport of big-game fishing.

By the mid-1890s, Holder had mastered the inshore fishery around Catalina and turned his attention to the vast schools of "leaping" tuna offshore. He marveled as these enormous predators hunted flying fish with complete abandon, often coming right into Avalon Harbor just a stone's throw from shore. Holder's determination to capture such a fish on rod and reel inspired others to take up the chase, and in 1896 Colonel C.P. Morehouse and W. Greer Campbell became the first two anglers to conquer the bluefin tuna (*Thunnus thynnus*) on balanced sporting tackle. A veteran tarpon fisherman, Morehouse experienced numerous broken rods, frozen reels, and snapped lines before finally succeeding in his quest. Two years later, Holder's capture of the first sizable tuna ever taken on sporting tackle – 183 lb – electrified the world and set the stage for the formation of the world's first big-game fishing organization: The Tuna Club of Santa Catalina Island.

After countless failures, Holder's capture of this 183 lb "leaping" tuna in 1898 made national news. The battle took four hours, during which the giant fish towed Holder's launch more than 10 miles.

19

The Mabel F. *enters Avalon Harbor in 1911 with a "leaping" tuna that took 17 hours to land. It was hooked at 2 p.m. on August 9th and did not surrender until 6:57 a.m. the following morning.*

PULLEY END RING

"BICKERDYKE" END RING

TOP RING

BRASS HEAD RING

Early saltwater guides came in many forms.

20

Immediately following his singular accomplishment, Holder gathered his like-minded friends and laid out what he had in mind for a new club. First and foremost, The Tuna Club was to serve as a standard-bearer for angling in its most elevated form. Only those few individuals who had taken a tuna in excess of 100 lb on sporting tackle were worthy of membership. All future members would be considered subject to this accomplishment, and strict new rules would apply to ensure the fairest possible battle between fish and fisherman. Indeed, the rules of engagement should favor neither party but rather allow each side an equal chance of success. In setting such high standards, Holder was also not unmindful of the long-term health of the fishery. Many fewer fish would be brought to gaff with rod and reel than with handlines, thereby protecting the resource for future generations of anglers.

Within the first sixty days, 24 men were successful in capturing their qualifying fish and were subsequently awarded The Tuna Club's blue button as a coveted symbol of membership. Due to the frequent state of exhaustion or injury that many anglers found themselves in after the battle, no signature was required at the time the catch was recorded into the Club's record book. The selection of Club officers was simple: whoever caught the largest tuna of the year automatically assumed the Presidency until such time as another member caught a larger fish. Holder's breakthrough catch earned him the

The Tuna Club's first clubhouse on Catalina Island, California.

Burned to cinders in the Avalon fire of 1915, The Tuna Club rebuilt its clubhouse the following year where it remains in use to this day.

title in 1898, but Col. Morehouse responded the following year with a 251 lb tuna that remains the Club's linen line record to this day. Early members were also responsible for many innovations in tackle and technique, including W.C. Boschen's prompting of reelmaker Julius vom Hofe to make the first saltwater reel suitable for big game, F.J. Rabbeth's invention of the externally adjustable drag, and J. A. Coxe's incorporation of same into a series of superior saltwater reels.

As The Tuna Club grew in membership and stature, its adherence to the highest standards of sportsmanship did not go unnoticed. Holder wrote feverishly about all aspects of California angling, but he was most eloquent in describing the sporting qualities of its saltwater species when taken on proper tackle. His numerous books and articles on angling were enormously influential during those most formative years, and his other works in the fields of natural history, biography, science, and education were as celebrated as any in their day. Among many other lasting accomplishments, Holder was also a founder of the venerable Valley Hunt Club in Pasadena and a co-founder of the world famous Tournament of Roses. He died in October of 1915 at his home in Pasadena, leaving behind an outdoor legacy of monumental proportions.

Tuna Club buttons.

Zane Grey's "pueblo" residence on Catalina was built in 1926 and remains an island landmark.

22

Holder's enthusiastic use of light tackle in the pursuit of large saltwater game fish created new standards for anglers everywhere.

During and after his tenure, The Tuna Club established many precedents that would come to guide the IGFA in its formation some 40 years hence. All innovations in tackle and technique were carefully weighed so that the angler would not gain an undue advantage over his quarry. When cable leader was first introduced in the early 1920s, its use quickly helped Club members set three new world records for broadbill swordfish. However, such leader also tended to envelop swordfish during the battle and frequently cut them to pieces. As a result, the use of cable leader was seen as reducing the sporting tendencies of the fish and subsequently banned. Other acts or omissions were also identified as disqualifying a catch from award consideration, including many that were later made part of the IGFA's first rule book.[9] In granting recognition to outstanding catches, much credit was given to captures on light tackle[10] and all members adhered to a strict set of rules that favored the fish as much as the fisherman. In those ways and countless others did The Tuna Club create the highest traditions of sportsmanship for the IGFA to follow.

---

[9] *For example, use of a broken rod, handlining a fish at any time, the participation of two or more anglers in the fight, etc.*

[10] *In 1906, Tuna Club member A.J. Eddy developed the concept of a lighter weight linen line, and two years later T.M. Potter conceived the famous "three-six" tackle standard by combining a six (6) oz rod of six (6) foot length with six (6)-thread line.*

Based largely on Holder's relentless promotion of the sport, tuna fishing slowly gained a following. By 1910, sporting tackle had improved to the point where anglers were challenging the giant bluefin tuna known to be off Nova Scotia,[11] and the first catch of substance came a year later when J.K.L. Ross landed a 680 lb specimen. In 1914, the dedicated British angler L. Mitchell-Henry took a pair of 500 lb tuna[12] in the same locale, and he was followed to the region 10 years later by Zane Grey. By that time a widely-acclaimed western author, Grey spent more than 20 years and a sizable fortune fishing for big game in various parts of the world. Tenacious, vindictive, uncharitable, he ultimately soured relations with almost every other big-game angler of his day, but Grey's eight books and numerous articles on angling introduced the sport to countless future enthusiasts. He was also a superb angler, setting many early records and combining with his brother R.C. to catch more than 40 swordfish off Catalina and elsewhere. Nevertheless, Grey's rod-and-reel capture of a 700 lb bluefin off Nova Scotia in 1924 was regarded largely as a stunt until others such as IGFA founder Michael Lerner arrived to duplicate the feat.

---

[11] In northeastern Canada.

[12] After losing 10 in a row.

23

Pioneering British angler L. Mitchell-Henry (left) discusses tackle with American author and sportsman Harlan Major in 1932.

Elsewhere, the first British "tunny" of substance was hooked and lost by Col. R.F.S. Cotton in 1930, but the erstwhile Mitchell-Henry succeeded later that year in capturing a 560 lb tuna some 60 miles off Scarborough in the North Sea. The weather was characteristically miserable, but British anglers persisted and the 1935 season saw 53 tuna with an average weight of 554 lb brought to the Scarborough dock. Giant tuna had also been found off Bimini in the Bahamas, where Francis Low made news with his catch of a 705 lb bluefin in 1933. Many other tuna were hooked and lost to the voracious local sharks, but legendary anglers Ernest Hemingway and Kip Farrington developed the technique of maintaining an angle between boat and fish to keep the fish away from deep-water predators. As a result, catch rates improved and Bimini went on to become one of the great blue water angling destinations of all time.

Although broadbill swordfish had been taken commercially off America's east coast since the 1840s, anglers remained cautious, mindful of reports of swordfish charging boats and piercing wooden hulls with their fearsome bills. Once again, the first sporting capture went to a Tuna Club member, this time to revered angler and sportsman W. C. Boschen in 1913. Aided

24

George Farnsworth (right) was one of Catalina's most able boatmen. Here he shows off his innovative fishing kite and one of the results it produced (ca. 1911).

by legendary Catalina boatman George Farnsworth,[13] Boschen made history with a swordfish of 355 lb, a catch so monumental that it was not duplicated in the Atlantic for another 14 years.[14] When Boschen died five years later, he left instructions for his ashes to be scattered over the swordfish grounds off Catalina by Farnsworth, and it was done.

The world's known assortment of billfish as illustrated by IGFA Trustee Guy Harvey.

One of the earliest big-game fish to be identified in ancient literature, the swordfish is unique among billfish for its enormous range and deep-water feeding ability. Swordfish are born with scales and teeth, but both disappear as the fish matures. While only a single genus/species classification has been identified, knowledge of swordfish ichthyology is extremely limited, due in part to the radically different appearance between juvenile and adult specimens. The swordfish is also highly unpredictable, adopting different behaviors in different locales, and is widely viewed as the toughest of all big-game fish to conquer. Since Boschen's first catch, a very few elite anglers such as Zane Grey,[15] Alfred C. Glassell Jr., Lou Marron, and IGFA Trustee Roy E. (Ted) Naftzger Jr. subsequently spent years in search of little else.

---

[13]*Farnsworth steered many prospective Tuna Club members to their qualifying buttons and developed the fishing kite along with many other angling innovations.*

[14]*The first swordfish taken on sporting tackle in the Atlantic is generally attributed to Oliver Grinnell who took a 193 lb specimen off Montauk in 1927.*

[15]*During his Catalina years, Grey focused largely on swordfish and was remarkably successful. He and his brother R.C. Grey combined for more than 40 swordfish, the largest being R.C.'s 588 lb catch. They fished from the Gladiator, a specially-built 52' cruiser that included 6' of cement in the hull to ward off incoming swordfish bills.*

5122. Sword Fish Caught at
Catalina Island, Calif.

As for the various species of marlin, the honor of the first rod-and-reel capture went to yet another Tuna Club member, E.B. Llewellyn, in 1903. Known off Catalina variously as "zebra fish," "belaying pin fish" and, more commonly, "marlin swordfish," the striped marlin (*Tetrapturus audax*) was an intermittent visitor to Island waters during the early years but proved to be a highly entertaining alternative to bluefin tuna. Indeed, when the tuna disappeared from Catalina waters for a period of years beginning in 1908, striped marlin became the game fish of choice among Tuna Club members. Although not as large as most other species of marlin, striped marlin are more acrobatically inclined and known for their spectacular aerial displays. In the Atlantic, a somewhat similar fishery for white marlin (*Tetrapturus albidus*) was pioneered off Ocean City, Maryland by brothers Paul and Jack Townsend. Nearly identical to the striped marlin, the somewhat smaller white marlin ranges some 40 degrees on either side of the Equator and quickly developed its own reputation as a sporting gamester of the highest order.

As the smaller marlin and sailfish became known to sportsmen, new techniques were developed to account for the difficulty in hooking these bony-mouthed fish. In Florida, fishing guide Charlie Thompson significantly improved his hook-up percentage by allowing sailfish to fully swallow the bait, and Captain Bill Hatch had early success using the underside of a bonito as strip bait. When combined, the drop-back-with-strip-bait technique proved to be deadly. Despite efforts to keep the new method a secret, other guides also discovered the idea and sailfish soon supplanted tarpon and kingfish as the most popular game species along Florida's east coast. Other new techniques were proving effective on a whole range of new species, including dorado, marlin, tuna, and wahoo. Soon a prosperous charter boat fleet was in place, tourists began flocking to the region, and the whole of southeast Florida boomed.

Miami's Chamber of Commerce Fishing Docks witnessed many early catches like this 82 lb Atlantic blue marlin taken in 1933.

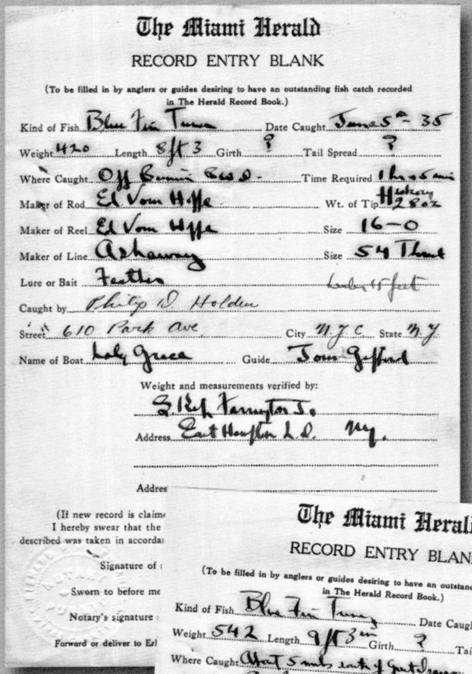

The Miami Herald
RECORD ENTRY BLANK

(To be filled in by anglers or guides desiring to have an outstanding fish catch recorded in The Herald Record Book.)

Kind of Fish **Blue Fin Tuna** Date Caught **June 5th 35**
Weight **420** Length **8 ft 3** Girth **?** Tail Spread **?**
Where Caught **Off Bimini B.W.I.** Time Required **1 hr 5 min**
Maker of Rod **Ed Vom Hofe** Wt. of Tip **Hickory 28 oz**
Maker of Reel **Ed Vom Hofe** Size **16-0**
Maker of Line **Ashaway** Size **54 Thread**
Lure or Bait **Feather** Leader 15 feet
Caught by **Philip D. Holden**
Street **610 Park Ave** City **N.Y.C.** State **N.Y.**
Name of Boat **Lady Grace** Guide **Tom Gifford**

Weight and measurements verified by:
S. Kip Farrington Jr.
Address **East Hampton L.I. N.Y.**

Address _____

(If new record is claimed...
I hereby swear that the...
described was taken in accordance...

Signature of ...

Sworn to before me ...

Notary's signature ...

Forward or deliver to Erl ...

The Miami Herald
RECORD ENTRY BLANK

(To be filled in by anglers or guides desiring to have an outstanding fish catch recorded in The Herald Record Book.)

Kind of Fish **Blue Fin Tuna** Date Caught **Thurs June 6th 1935**
Weight **542** Length **9 ft 3** Girth **?** Tail Spread **?**
Where Caught **About 5 miles east of Great Isaac** Time Required **3 hr 40 min**
Maker of Rod **Ed Vom Hofe** Wt. of Tip **28 oz**
Maker of Reel **Ed Vom Hofe** Size **16-0**
Maker of Line **Ashaway** Size **54 Thread**
Lure or Bait **Feather** Leader 15 feet
Caught by **S. Kip Farrington**
Street **East Hampton L.I.** City **N.Y.** State
Name of Boat **Lady Grace** Guide **Capt Tom Gifford**

Weight and measurements verified by:
Louis R. Ripley
Address **26 East 81st NYC**

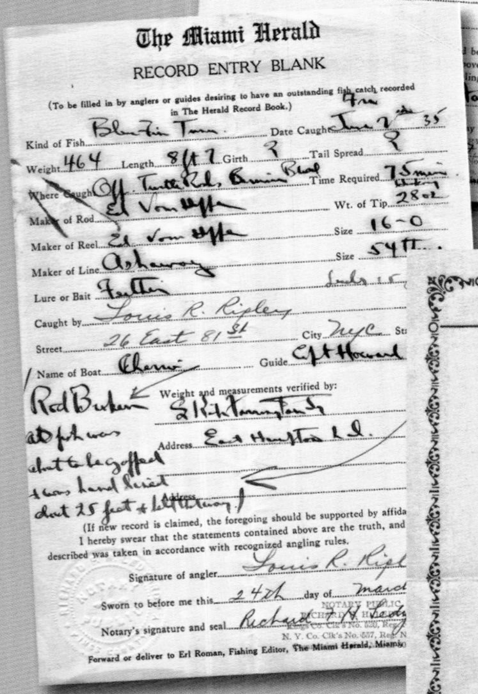

The Miami Herald
RECORD ENTRY BLANK

(To be filled in by anglers or guides desiring to have an outstanding fish catch recorded in The Herald Record Book.)

Kind of Fish **Blue Fin Tuna** Date Caught **Tues June 2nd 35**
Weight **464** Length **8 ft 7** Girth **?** Tail Spread **?**
Where Caught **Off Turtle Rks, Bimini Bank** Time Required **75 min**
Maker of Rod **Ed Vom Hofe** Wt. of Tip **28 oz**
Maker of Reel **Ed Vom Hofe** Size **16-0**
Maker of Line **Ashaway** Size **54 Thread**
Lure or Bait **Feather** Leader 18
Caught by **Louis R. Ripley**
Street **26 East 81st** City **NYC** State
Name of Boat **Cherri** Guide **Capt Howell**

Rod Broken
at first was ...
went to be gaffed ...
was hand lined ...
about 25 feet & left strong)

(If new record is claimed, the foregoing should be supported by affidavit.
I hereby swear that the statements contained above are the truth, and
described was taken in accordance with recognized angling rules.

Signature of angler **Louis R. Ripley**
Sworn to before me this **24th** day of **March**
Notary's signature and seal **Robert ...**
N.Y. Co. Clk's No. 557, Reg. N...
Forward or deliver to Erl Roman, Fishing Editor, The Miami Herald, Miami

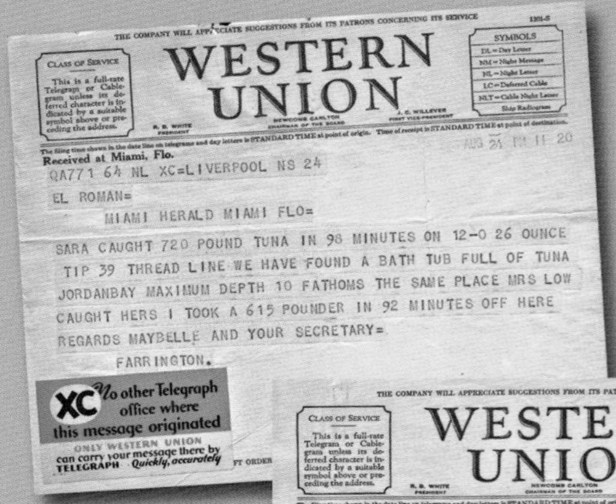

(middle column overflow from second form)

...be supported by affidavit.)
...are the truth, and that the fish
...ing rules.

...rrington
...of **March** 1936
...Y PUBLIC
...H. Ledyard
...67, Reg. No. 71,358
...Herald, Miami, Florida.

WESTERN UNION

Received at Miami, Flo.
QA771 64 NL XC=LIVERPOOL NS 24

EL ROMAN=
MIAMI HERALD MIAMI FLO=

SARA CAUGHT 720 POUND TUNA IN 98 MINUTES ON 12-0 26 OUNCE
TIP 39 THREAD LINE WE HAVE FOUND A BATH TUB FULL OF TUNA
JORDANBAY MAXIMUM DEPTH 10 FATHOMS THE SAME PLACE MRS LOW
CAUGHT HERS I TOOK A 615 POUNDER IN 92 MINUTES OFF HERE
REGARDS MAYBELLE AND YOUR SECRETARY=
FARRINGTON.

XC No other Telegraph office where this message originated

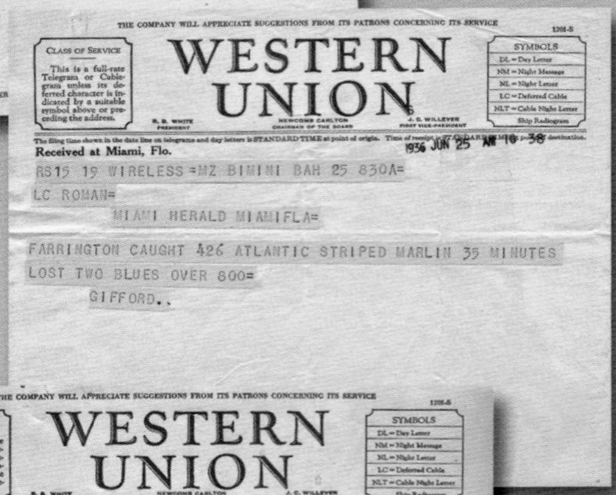

WESTERN UNION

Received at Miami, Flo.
RS15 19 WIRELESS =MZ BIMINI BAH 25 830A=

LC ROMAN=
MIAMI HERALD MIAMI FLA=

FARRINGTON CAUGHT 426 ATLANTIC STRIPED MARLIN 35 MINUTES
LOST TWO BLUES OVER 800=
GIFFORD.

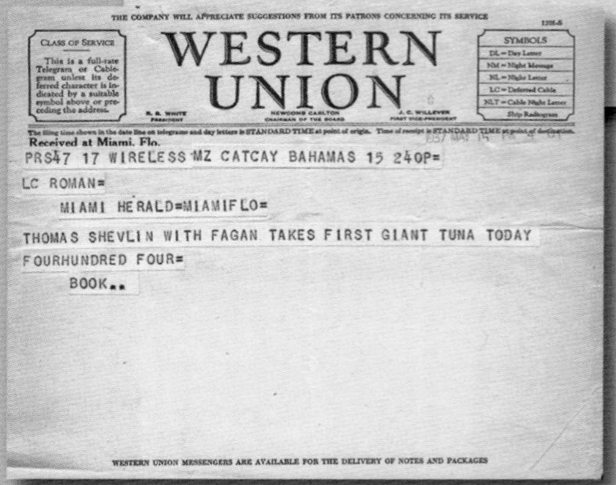

WESTERN UNION

Received at Miami, Flo.
PRS47 17 WIRELESS MZ CATCAY BAHAMAS 15 240P=

LC ROMAN=
MIAMI HERALD=MIAMIFLO=

THOMAS SHEVLIN WITH FAGAN TAKES FIRST GIANT TUNA TODAY
FOURHUNDRED FOUR=
BOOK..

WESTERN UNION MESSENGERS ARE AVAILABLE FOR THE DELIVERY OF NOTES AND PACKAGES

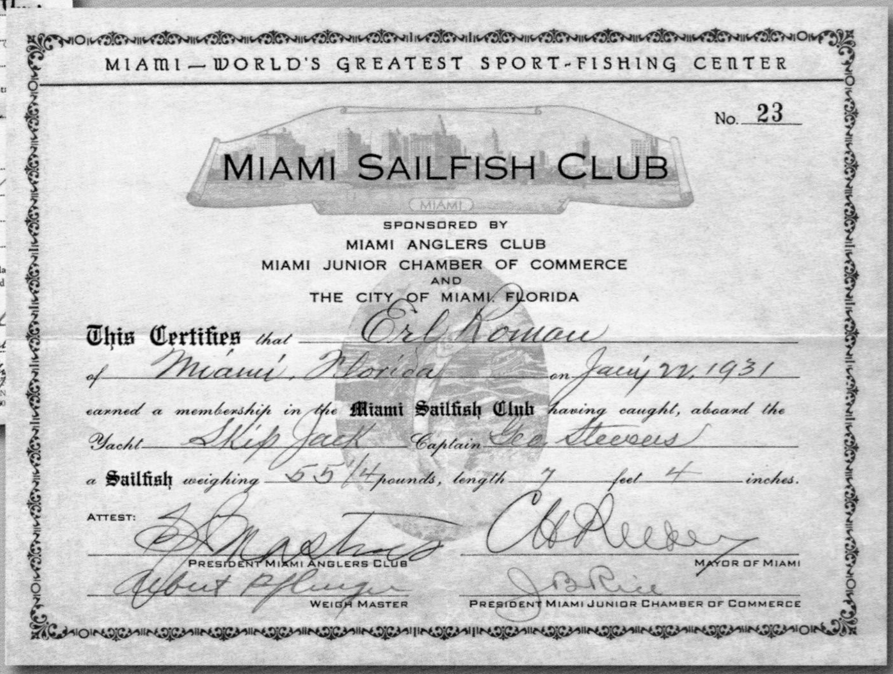

MIAMI—WORLD'S GREATEST SPORT-FISHING CENTER

No. **23**

MIAMI SAILFISH CLUB
(MIAMI)

SPONSORED BY
MIAMI ANGLERS CLUB
MIAMI JUNIOR CHAMBER OF COMMERCE
AND
THE CITY OF MIAMI FLORIDA

This Certifies that _**Erl Roman**_
of _**Miami, Florida**_ on _**Jan'y 22, 1931**_
earned a membership in the **Miami Sailfish Club** having caught, aboard the
Yacht _**Skip Jack**_ Captain _**Fo Stevens**_
a **Sailfish** weighing _**55¼**_ pounds, length _**7**_ feet _**4**_ inches.

ATTEST:

_____ _____
PRESIDENT MIAMI ANGLERS CLUB MAYOR OF MIAMI

Albert Pflueger _____
WEIGH MASTER PRESIDENT MIAMI JUNIOR CHAMBER OF COMMERCE

Telegrams and catch certificates like these gave proof of the booming Florida fishery. Note the many well-known anglers, including Kip Farrington, Al Pflueger, Erl Roman, and Tommy Shevlin.

28

By the 1930s, fishing for big game had exploded in popularity. Summer runs of giant bluefin had been discovered off Bimini, and Prohibition-era travelers came to drink and fish. In 1935, Ernest Hemingway was the first to land a giant bluefin untouched by sharks, capturing a 315 lb fish on his boat *Pilar*. Early anglers such as Frank O'Brien, Julio Sanchez, and Tommy Shevlin built lasting reputations there, and charter boat skippers such as Bill Fagen and Tommy Gifford were in constant demand. Later IGFA personalities also began to surface, including S. Kip Farrington, Van Campen Heilner, and Michael Lerner. All three helped to pioneer the Bahamas fishery, and the first few years were a magical blend of tremendous fishing, manly camaraderie, and a great sense of adventure.

Captain Bill Fagen's legendary charter boat Florida Cracker II. *Fagen is at bottom left.*

Zane Grey with a trio of black, blue, and "silver" marlin taken in Tahiti (ca. 1932).

As anglers began to range farther offshore, reports began to trickle in of encounters with larger blue and black marlin. The Atlantic blue marlin *(Makaira nigricans)* was first noted by science in 1802 when a large specimen washed ashore after a storm in the Bay of Biscay.[16] The fish became dinner for the locals but a sketch and description found their way to interested naturalists in London. In 1837, another sizable example surfaced near the Cape of Good Hope and was ultimately shipped to the British Museum for inspection. That fish caused more confusion than enlightenment, and it remains an open question to this day as to the exact relationship between the Atlantic and Pacific blue marlin *(Makaira mazara)*. While H.L. Woodward's pioneering rod-and-reel catch of an Atlantic blue marlin off Cuba in 1922 paved the way for eastern sportsmen, it wasn't until George Parker's defining catch off Hawaii in 1954 that the Pacific blue marlin was formally recognized. Before that, the species was variously known as "Tahitian black" or silver marlin, and records were kept for one or both nonexistent species for many years. Especially noteworthy was Zane Grey's capture of a 1,040 lb "silver" marlin off Tahiti in 1930, the first thousand-pound landing of any game fish despite its being mutilated by sharks. It would take another 22 years before the first unmutilated marlin over one thousand pounds would be landed according to IGFA rules.

In the meantime, the discovery of big marlin and tuna off Bimini and Cay Cay gave a further surge to Florida's charter boat operators. Those rich fishing grounds were easily within reach of game boats operating from

---

[16] *A large Atlantic inlet shared by France and Spain.*

Miami's legendary Pier 5, and the establishment of shore-based hospitality outposts at both islands added a new dimension. Big-game tackle had also improved dramatically from just 10 years before, but it was still far from perfect and catastrophic failures in the heat of battle were common. Nevertheless, a trend towards lighter tackle surfaced as the sport continued to evolve, enabling less hearty anglers to do battle with giant fish. If big-game angling still entailed a lot of hard work, it was neither as back-breaking nor as dangerous as before.

The advent of big-game angling tournaments also did much to publicize the sport. While contests such as the International Tuna Cup Matches in Wedgeport and the Cat Cay Tuna Tournament were limited entry events, the founding of the Metropolitan Miami Fishing Tournament (the MET) in 1936 was another story. Conceived by 39 community leaders,[17] the event was open to all comers and offered awards in dozens of different categories. By 1939, the MET was attracting an incredible 104,000 participants over its 90-day run, including contestants from 38 states and seven foreign countries. Tournament results were featured on local and national radio and in dozens of different publications. A census of Florida visitors taken that year indicated that 70% had come primarily for the fishing. Not only was recreational angling adding some $200 million per year to local coffers, but it was also adding to the number of permanent Florida residents. By the late 1930s, fishing had surpassed even the Orange Bowl in its importance to Florida's economy.

In America and beyond, big-game fishing had suddenly become big business. What was needed now was an element of control.

31

---

[17]Including Miami Herald *columnist Erl Roman, about whom much will be said later.*

Florida's Metropolitan Miami Fishing Tournament included a ceremonial boat parade and considerable pageantry.

Michael Lerner, 1941.

Chapter Two

MICHAEL LERNER AND THE FOUNDING OF THE IGFA

The old adage that "success has many fathers" holds little truth when it comes to the International Game Fish Association. Indeed, that the IGFA can trace its founding back to a single man is an indisputable fact. Without Michael Lerner's energy, vision, financial capacity and angling reputation, the IGFA would never have been formed on the eve of World War II and endured as it has for more than 65 years. No other individual would put forth a claim even as co-founder. All of the original parties involved deferred to Lerner throughout their tenure and always knew him to be the driving force behind the organization. From the IGFA's founding in 1939 to his resignation as President in 1961, Michael Lerner was the heart and soul of the IGFA.

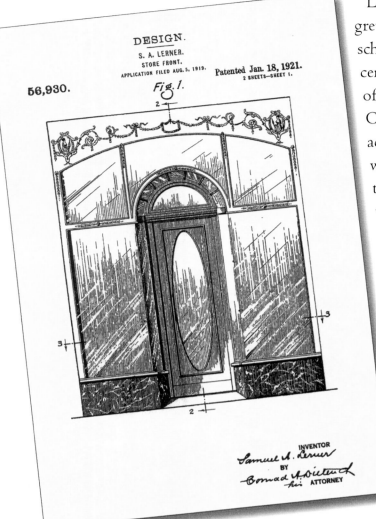

This distinctive facade for the Lerner Shops was trademarked by Sam Lerner in 1921.

Lerner was born in Philadelphia in 1890 and grew up in New York City. During his public school years, he may have noted the turn-of-the-century headlines extolling the remarkable catches of giant tuna being made off Catalina Island in California. In any event, while Lerner's own early accomplishments were unexceptional, his father would take him fishing in Sheepshead Bay where they caught porgy and other groundfish. Those were surely formative days, but no one could have predicted this middle son of a large rough-and-tumble family would become what the *New York Times* described in 1943 as "the world's outstanding deep sea angler."

By 1917, Woodrow Wilson was in office, America had entered the Great War, and "Mike" Lerner was a sturdy 26-year-old desk-bound Army sergeant anxious to get on with his life. Upon completing his military service, he became a traveling salesman for his brother Sam's wholesale dry goods business. As the firm grew, the brothers began to entertain the idea of opening retail outlets, and the Lorraine (later Lerner) Shops were founded on the wave of a booming post-war economy. Along with his father and two brothers, Mike Lerner threw himself into the retail business and for the next 18 years worked tirelessly to make the enterprise a success. Along the way, he held many positions within the firm and was widely credited with being its most vital executive.

In 1921, Lerner was further buoyed when he met and married Helen Samuels, a petite and elegant young woman of breeding who would prove to have every bit the taste for adventure as her husband. At barely 5' tall and 110 lb, she was an almost comical contrast to her burly spouse, but it proved to be an ideal match and they were devoted to each other for more than 50 years. Later photographs of Helen among her many big-game conquests would invariably show her as sleek and elegant with her hair pulled back in a tight bun. Prone to seasickness, she was nevertheless an outstanding offshore angler and established a number of milestones for women in both fishing and hunting. Their happy union was one of the great sporting partnerships of all time.

By the time he was 40, Lerner was already a wealthy man and had begun to lose interest in the frenetic pace of business. Despite the looming Depression, he turned management of the firm over to his brother and retired for good, roaming the world with Helen in pursuit of the sporting life. Under family tutelage, the business continued to grow and by 1945 the firm's annual sales had reached $87 million. Ultimately, more than 470 Lerner specialty apparel stores dotted the landscape at the time of Lerner's death, leaving him in his twilight years with the quiet satisfaction of an enduring vocational legacy.

Helen and Mike Lerner in Bimini.

The Anchorage - the Lerners' Bimini home (ca. 1937).

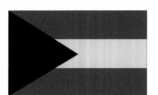

Flag of the Bahamas.

Soon after their marriage, Helen and Mike Lerner began what would become a new life of fulfillment and accomplishment in search of big game.[1] At first it was hunting, and their New York apartment came to be crowded with trophy animals from Africa and beyond. Nevertheless, Lerner's experience in catching a 70 lb Atlantic bluefin tuna off Long Island in the early 1920s was an epiphany. He was stunned by the strength and power of such a fish, and later success with tarpon off Key West prompted both Lerners to take up serious big-game fishing during the early 1930s. After hearing stories about giant tuna and marlin traveling virtually unmolested along the Bimini shoreline, their subsequent visit to that tropical paradise would change their lives.

About the time of the Lerners' arrival, Bimini was just beginning to stir from years of benign neglect. In 1920, author and sportsman Van Campen Heilner set up a crude beach camp in Bimini and began to fish, at first primarily for bonefish but occasionally venturing offshore. An experienced angler, he nevertheless lost battle after battle with local monsters until finally catching a pair of small blue marlin in 1925. In the meantime, he became captivated by the island's spectacular beauty and was warmed by the hospitality of its 250 black natives. Loathe for years to put out the word on his private sanctuary, Heilner finally relented and extended a few quiet invitations to personal friends. The Lerners were among the first to arrive, and Bimini quickly became their tropical home for all future endeavors.

During the early 1930s, Helen and Mike fished avidly off Bimini and both soon established reputations as superior anglers. Warmly welcomed by the natives and also much taken by the scenic vistas, they built a sizable home shaped like a ship on the island's north shore that they

---

[1] They had no children.

christened "the Anchorage." One of its most distinctive features was a "crow's nest" hideaway on top to accommodate such frequent guests as Ernest Hemingway.[2] In turn, the Lerners endeared themselves to the local population in 1935 when they quickly responded with aid after a devastating hurricane. By this time, the sensational game fishing to be had off Bimini was no secret, and they regularly played host to such legendary anglers as Hemingway, Kip Farrington, Tommy Shevlin, Julio Sanchez, and Erl Roman. Life was good, and it would only get better.

---

[2]*Indeed, Mike Lerner became a great and good friend of Hemingway, helping him with his investments and facilitating the paperwork surrounding a Bimini property that Hemingway tried to buy. Hemingway responded with many warm letters covering the looming war in Europe, fishing off Cat Cay, and always his great appreciation of Lerner's friendship.*

An impressive quartet of blue marlin taken off Bimini in 1935. From left are Ernest Hemingway, Captain Archie Cass and mate Carlos from the "Pilar", Mike Lerner, Captain Tommy Gifford from Lerner's boat "Lady Grace", Captain Fred Lister from the vessel "Willow D." (owned by Cuban sugar magnate Julio Sanchez), and mate.

Mike Lerner hooked up aboard a Wedgeport dory in 1935. Such vessels offered few creature comforts to the angler.

By now firmly ensconced in Bimini and anxious to explore new waters, Mike Lerner decided in 1935 to venture north to Canada to try his hand at giant tuna fishing. That summer, he and renowned Florida fishing guide Tommy Gifford fished Liverpool and nearby Jordan Bay in Nova Scotia, but without success. In phoning Helen in New York to report the bad news, Lerner was overheard by a traveling salesman who told him there were tuna to be had in Wedgeport (Yarmouth County) about 70 miles to the southwest. With that, Gifford and Lerner headed off to Wedgeport the next day where they arranged for a homemade fighting chair to be mounted in a small dory. Their subsequent capture of two giant tuna the following day on rod and reel astounded the 1,700 townspeople. Such fish, it was thought, could never be taken except by harpoon.

Mike Lerner shows off a sensational catch of Atlantic bluefin tuna taken off Wedgeport in 1935.

After a subsequent eight days of spectacular fishing during which Lerner landed another 21 of the huge fish (known locally as "horse mackerel"), he gathered together a group of influential locals for a meeting at the nearby town hall. To a dubious audience, he described Wedgeport as an undiscovered angling mecca that would soon attract big-game enthusiasts from all corners of the world. He would put the word out, Lerner told the locals, and they needed to get ready. Clean your lobster boats, put in a fighting chair, and buy some fishing tackle. The world was coming, and soon.

A bronze souvenir tuna from the 1958 International Tuna Cup Matches held in Wedgeport.

Lerner was as good as his word. By the next year (1936), American anglers were already a demanding presence in town. To accommodate the heretofore non-existent tourists, the startled town scrambled to arrange hospitality. Grateful for the respite from commercial fishing, local fishermen put away their harpoon gear and bought the largest reels they could find.[3] Soon an association was formed on behalf of Wedgeport boatmen, and boats were offered for charter at the impressive rate of $25 per day. When Lerner invited noted angler Kip Farrington and his wife Chisie to sample the tuna fishing, the couple was astounded at the abundance and proximity of these enormous fish. More than 100 giant tuna were caught in Wedgeport that season, and the first of the International Tuna Cup Matches (better known as the Sharp Cup) was held the following year.

39

---

[3]*The first were so-called Balboa reels, but when it became apparent that they couldn't stand up to the strain, the locals went to Hardy/Zane Grey and later Penn reels in 12/0 and 14/0 sizes.*

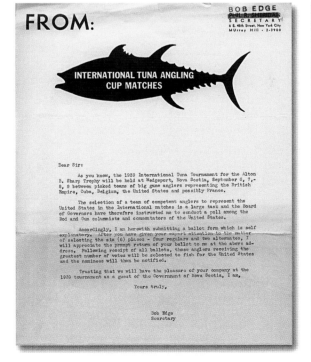

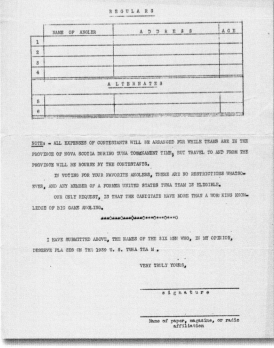

A 1939 letter and ballot from Sharp Cup Secretary Bob Edge soliciting nominations for the American team.

AMNH ichthyologist Francesca LaMonte.

By now extensively traveled, Lerner was also beginning to recognize how little was known about the ocean and its creatures. The scientific world was convinced that life first began in the oceanic depths, but almost nothing was known about marine flora and fauna. Lerner was also startled by the woeful lack of research facilities dedicated to marine studies. While enormous sums were being spent to study the heavens, the science of oceanic life was attracting little interest. Resolving to do what he could to rectify the situation, he began in 1935 by donating a mounted blue marlin taken off Bimini to the American Museum of Natural History in New York. Accepting the gift on behalf of the Museum was a diminutive young staff ichthyologist named Francesca LaMonte. Exceedingly bright, highly educated, "Fran" was a rising star at the Museum and one of only five female ichthyologists in the world at that time. Improbably, the two became mutual admirers and comrades-in-arms, leading to a devoted 40-year friendship that would benefit both parties beyond measure.[4]

Lerner's generous donation had also piqued the interest of the American Museum of Natural History, one of the most somber and august institutions of its day. The AMNH was founded in the mid-1800s by the best New York families as a suitable place to display their personal trophies and collections. Built around an existing armory in Central Park,

40

---

[4] *Always formal, the two invariably addressed each other as Miss LaMonte and Mr. Lerner.*

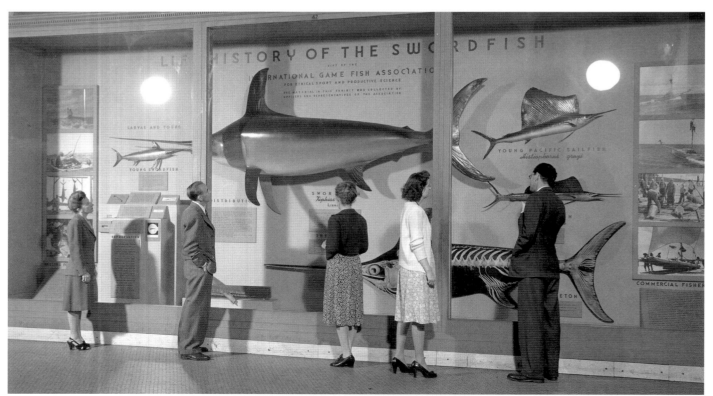

Lerner's many gifts prompted the AMNH to create the Hall of Fishes of the World, long one of its most popular displays.

The Museum's certificate
of appreciation presented to
Lerner, the first of many.

Mike Lerner admires his gift to the AMNH (1935).

the Museum ultimately covered 24 acres and grew to include an extensive
exhibition of marine life. Lerner's blue marlin was the first of many more
gifts that followed, and his subsequent organization and sponsorship of six
expeditions on behalf of the Museum added enormously to its institutional
luster. Ultimately, Lerner's establishment of the world famous Lerner
Marine Laboratory on Bimini would provide an unprecedented research
platform for the Museum. In return, the AMNH reciprocated by naming
him a Trustee in 1941, and their unqualified support of a fledgling IGFA
two years before would prove to be crucial.

(l–r) Mike Lerner, Captain Tommy Gifford, and mate Larry Bagby watch as a swordfish comes aboard their mothership in Nova Scotia, 1936.

Planning for the first Lerner expedition in 1936 was already well underway when Lerner made an off-hand comment to Dr. William Gregory[5] that Museum scientists would be welcome to tag along. Six staffers ultimately accompanied that first voyage and set the tone for what would evolve into five years of unprecedented public/private exploration. Returning to Nova Scotia, Lerner's first expedition during the summer of 1936 lasted about a month and focused on the rich swordfish grounds off Cape Breton. Lerner made all the arrangements and paid all the bills for the 10 participants. As with his subsequent expeditions, this one added much to the existing knowledge of big-game species by providing multiple fresh specimens for dissection and study. First-ever data on migratory and feeding habits, breeding grounds, growth characteristics, and other variables were also gleaned, and Lerner himself became a most capable assistant to the Museum ichthyologists.

Big-game anglers had long been aware of the tremendous swordfish density off Cape Breton, as commercial swordfish efforts in the height of the season often resulted in more than 150 fish per day. This first expedition was based in Louisburg, Nova Scotia, Canada's easternmost point before Newfoundland. If the town wasn't much, at least the scenery

---

[5] *Then Chairman of both the Ichthyology and Comparative Anatomy Departments at the Museum, plus a Professor of Paleontology at Columbia University.*

was breathtaking. Louisburg's 800 year-round residents were a hardy bunch and almost wholly reliant on commercial swordfishing for their livelihood. However, the fish were invariably cleaned at sea and returned to the dock in ready-for-market condition, lacking the head, entrails, and careful handling needed for scientific evaluation. Lerner fished from a dory along with Captain Tommy Gifford and crew, and on August 3rd he met with record success in boating the first rod-and-reel swordfish ever taken off Nova Scotia.[6] As it happened, the weather was horrendous even in the summer, and Lerner was able to fish only four days during the entire month. Nevertheless, during those four days he presented baits to 16 fish, obtained 14 strikes, hooked 10, broke off two, pulled the hook on five, and landed three: sensational results under the circumstances.

In a letter to Hemingway written during the trip, Lerner gushed that on a flat day the ocean "was covered with swordfish", and he estimated that 60% of the swordfish sighted offshore weighed 500 lb or more. Mackerel was the bait of choice, and Lerner's experience of evincing so many swordfish to strike was in sharp contrast to the frustrating indifference that swordfish elsewhere often showed for hooked baits. These swordfish were big, plentiful, and hungry, and anglers in search of this ultimate game fish would flock to Louisburg in the coming years.

With one swordfish already aboard, Mike Lerner battles a second off Louisburg.

43

---

[6] *The fish weighed 462.5 lbs.*

The Vigilant, *one of Louisburg's commercial swordfish boats newly rigged for rod-and-reel angling.*

GUEST REGISTER

DATE	NAME - RESIDENCE	REMARKS	CAME ABOARD AT
July 4 1936 July 8 '36	Pauline Hemingway Ernest Hemingway Chisie Farrington	thanks for a month of heaven with love to Helen and Mike and thank you for a lovely summer The perfect Anchorage with the perfect couple The best place to stay and the finest invitation a man could have. Bimini was never the same before.	Dawn – Stayed 4 weeks! June 7 stayed very happily! Courtney
"	S. Kip Farrington Jr.		
July 12	Don Stillman	Greetings to two charter members of the Bahamian marlin and Tuna Club from the vice-president of the Bimini Baracuda Club.	July 7.

The Lerners' guest registry from their Bimini home included many great angling names of the era. Frequent visitors included Ernest Hemingway, Chisie and Kip Farrington, columnist Erl Roman, Cuban angling great Julio Sanchez, artist Lynn Bogue Hunt, and steel cable magnate Ferdinand Roebling.

44

GUEST REGISTER

ATE	NAME - RESIDENCE	REMARKS	CAME ABOARD AT
ly 5	Ed. Roman - "Ye Fishing Editor"	Who owes his first blue marlin to Mike and Helen Lerner - not to mention a week of wonderful piscatorial pleasure! = Thanks a Million! =	
ly 5	Maybelle Roman	I came because I was invited, and stayed because I loved it - Who wouldn't?	
ly 7	Julie Sanchez	I hope you get a fish so big that I can use it for bait.	
ly 8	Lynn Bogue Hunt	Three Blue Marlin in three days - Gawd what a Woman Helen is!	How too Mike you Ol' Rascal
ly 8	Irene Severs	Besides being a great fisher, and a sweet gal, Helen makes one feel that Bimini is a Metropolis in the ocean	
ly 8	Ferdie Roehling	Most wonderful hospitality and what not heef - here's to this anchorage!	

I WISH THESE LERNERS WOULD MOVE AWAY LYNN BOGUE HUNT

Bob - N. Y.

Two smaller expeditions followed that initial effort: first to Bimini in 1937 and then back to Cape Breton the following year to clear up some minor uncertainties. Logistics for the Bimini trip were modest as Lerner established a temporary laboratory in his home and returned daily with fresh specimens from local waters. Smaller fish were opportunistically collected as available, and examples were returned to the Museum in a hodge-podge of jars and boxes. Many on-site molds were also taken in preparation for eventual castings. Helen Lerner proved to be inexhaustible in cataloguing photographs, and significant results included new data on blue marlin along with the first outline of what would later become the Lerner Marine Laboratory.

Things once again got complicated with the large Australia/New Zealand Expedition in 1939. As before, Lerner underwrote the entire production at enormous personal expense, and both he and Helen contributed countless hours in making the logistical arrangements. The expedition's considerable

The crew of Lerner's second Cape Breton Expedition, 1938. Standing at left are Francesca LaMonte and Mike Lerner, with Helen Lerner admiring the day's catch at right. Among the kneeling crew are Larry Bagby (2nd from left) and Tommy Gifford (with camera).

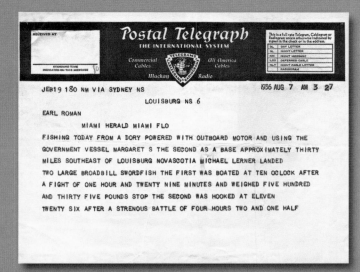
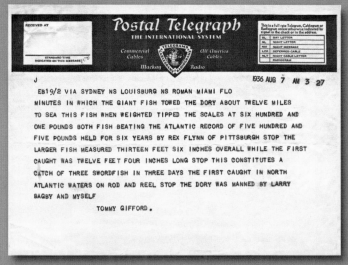

A two-page telegram from Tommy Gifford to Erl Roman advising him of the sensational fishing off Louisburg (1936).

scientific and photographic staff traveled by boat via Hawaii and Fiji and returned with a number of rare specimens. More significantly, Lerner was introduced to Clive Firth, a successful Sydney businessman and co-founder of the Bermagui Big Game Anglers' Club. Firth was a stout man with thinning brown hair: not exactly a picture of health but a passionate and accomplished angler nonetheless. Firth had also recently been elected President of the New South Wales Rod Fishers' Society, an influential group founded in 1904 and now just beginning to recognize the enormous potential that big-game angling held for Australia. The two men hit it off immediately and found themselves with much to talk about.

Two years before, Australian anglers had gathered in Sydney in an attempt to unify the rules and ethics relative to their budding sport. Held on a promising spring day in late October of 1937, the group consisted of representatives from four of Australia's five major regions.[7] Clive Firth was appointed the organization's first chairman, and the group adopted the name Game Fishing Association of Australia (GFAA) the following year.[8] Having reviewed the existing rules and knowing full well their incompleteness and inadequacy, Chairman Firth drafted an entirely new foundation for the sport that delineated such things as line classes and allowable tackle. By the following year (1938), Firth had broadened his thinking and recognized a worldwide need for a comprehensive angling standard. Endorsed by the GFAA membership, he approached the British Tunny Club to help establish such regulations, but they were unable to agree on a suitably objective governing body that would satisfy all parties. Frustrated and distracted by the looming world war, Firth returned to Australia to brood and scheme.

---

[7] The representative from South Australia could not attend.
[8] The organization continues to this day.

Mike Lerner, Clive Firth, and Helen Lerner in Australia (1939).

Flag of Australia.

Finally in 1939, Firth saw his chance. Contacted by Lerner in early 1939 to help with the upcoming expedition, he willingly organized the facilities needed by the scientific team (including a full lab) and fished extensively with Lerner during his stay. At every opportunity, Firth reviewed his ideas with Lerner, Gregory, and other expedition participants and urged them to begin such an organization. The fact was that while the sport of big-game angling was spreading rapidly across the globe, there was no central clearinghouse for information. While some pioneering anglers were more interested in doing their own exploring than reading second-hand accounts,[9] others were calling for an international body to coordinate angler interaction and begin filling in the many looming gaps in marine science. The seven seas were much more difficult to investigate than land, and even such basic science as identification of the major billfish species had not been perfected. Firth saw all that and more, and he implored Lerner to create an American standard for all to follow.

---

[9]*Most notably, Zane Grey in the early 1920s and Alfred C. Glassell Jr. some 30 years later.*

Intrigued, Lerner continued on with his expedition to New Zealand and Fiji where further discussions ensued. After being urged on by noted New Zealand angler Dr. Harold Pettit and others, Gregory was the first to grow enthused and suggested that the AMNH might be willing to affiliate itself with such an effort. By now, Lerner could see the possibilities and upon returning home sent a flurry of letters to fellow anglers, tackle dealers, fishing clubs, and other parties to gauge the level of interest in forming such an entity. Despite the growing war, the response was wildly enthusiastic as many anglers had been frustrated by a lack of standardized rules and records with which to measure their own fishing success. Saltwater records of a sort had been kept for some years by the outdoor magazine *Field & Stream*, but *F & S* Fishing Editor Dan Holland recognized their lack of rigor and was quick to endorse the idea of a dedicated record-keeper. Buoyed by that response and with the support of the American Museum of Natural History in his pocket, Lerner was quick to act.

Early angling pins awarded by Field & Stream.

Expedition crates are loaded from New Zealand's Mayor Island for shipment back to New York.

THE AMERICAN MUSEUM OF NATURAL HISTORY
NEW YORK

October the twenty-first
Nineteen hundred thirty-six

Dear Sir:

I have the pleasure to advise you that, at a meeting of the Executive Committee of The American Museum of Natural History, held on October 15, 1936, the following resolution was unanimously adopted:

RESOLVED, That, in accordance with the recommendation of the Director and Curator William K. Gregory, the Trustees take pleasure in appointing Mr. Michael Lerner Field Associate in the Department of Ichthyology, in recognition of his generous and continuous interest in the department's work.

Very truly yours,

Executive Secretary.

Mr. Michael Lerner,
C/o Lerner Stores Corp.,
354 - 4th Avenue,
New York City.

50

The inaugural meeting of the International Game Fish Association took place on June 7th, 1939 in a cramped upstairs office at the AMNH. In attendance were Gregory, Museum ichthyologists Francesca LaMonte and John Nichols, author Van Campen Heilner, and Lerner. At Lerner's insistence, Gregory was elected IGFA's first President with Lerner accepting a Vice Presidency and Frannie LaMonte assuming the role of Secretary. An Executive Committee of Lerner, Gregory, Heilner, and LaMonte was also created, and this group would form the IGFA's nucleus throughout its early years. With the formalities resolved, Lerner announced that he would personally underwrite all expenses of the new organization, a level of support he would continue to maintain until his resignation as IGFA President in 1961. For his contributions, Firth was selected as the IGFA's first International Representative.[10] Just like that, the IGFA was underway.

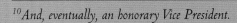

[10]*And, eventually, an honorary Vice President.*

The following year, Lerner mounted yet another expedition, this one to the virtually unexplored waters off Chile and Peru. Accompanying the Lerners were two fishing guides, four photographers, a number of scientific staffers (including the ubiquitous Frannie), and 162 pieces of luggage.[11] Two boats loaded with personnel and equipment left Miami and made the long voyage south, first settling in Talara, Peru and then relocating to Tocopilla, Chile. The goal of the expedition was to study billfish (especially swordfish) in their home waters, and much work was accomplished despite relatively poor fishing. Swordfish were scarce in Peru that season, with expedition boats ranging far and wide with no results. Finally, two nice specimens were taken at night,[12] with great interim entertainment provided by the frequent incidental captures of Humboldt squid to 75 lb.

[11] *The camera equipment alone occupied one entire stateroom.*
[12] *Weighing 380 and 620 lb.*

Lerner and crew battle giant Humboldt squid at night. The hoods provided only partial protection from the squid's sticky black ink.

Helen Lerner and Captain Bill Hatch prepare to back down on a fish during the 1940 Peru-Chile Expedition. Note the movie camera atop the bridge.

While swordfish may have been in short supply, the same could not be said of striped marlin. Throughout the trip, the marlin were so thick as to be considered pestilential, and no lines were trolled due to their constant annoyance. Scientific examinations of those and many other species were conducted late into the night, with Helen coordinating the activity and Mike participating on all fronts. While fishing in Chile proved little better, the expedition returned to Miami with detailed measurements of nearly four dozen marlin and swordfish, plus miscellaneous biological samples, reams of data, 38,000 feet of film, and more than 4,000 photographs. Already adorned with an academic title[13] to go with his many other accomplishments, Lerner could now bask in the glow of real scientific achievement.

[13]*Field Associate of Ichthyology of the American Museum of Natural History.*

Lerner assists Francesca LaMonte in dissecting a billfish in Peru.

A nice fish comes aboard for Mike Lerner and crew Doug Osborn during the Peru-Chile Expedition.

Aerial view of the Anchorage (at top of photo) and the Lerner Marine Laboratory in Bimini (ca. 1948).

Mike Lerner would mount one more small expedition the following year (1941), traveling to Ecuador with scientist Henry Raven to resolve discrepancies noted during the previous trip. Regrettably, World War II brought such excursions to an end, so Lerner turned his attention back to Bimini and what would become a major priority in conjunction with the AMNH: development of the Lerner Marine Laboratory. Lerner's contributions to the Museum had already been pivotal in allowing the Museum to expand its signature Hall of Fishes gallery, and veterans of the Lerner expeditions were keenly aware of the value of uninterrupted field work. When Lerner once again approached the Museum, this time about the feasibility of establishing a permanent field station on Bimini, Dr. Charles Breder Jr. was sent to investigate the idea. After a day-long tour, Breder was dazzled by the possibilities, and serious planning for the laboratory began that night.

Laboratory research vessels would alight at the pier and deposit their live specimens into these holding pens.

Helen Lerner watches a giant tuna come aboard off Brittany (1947).

Located 50 miles east of Miami, the island of Bimini was already known to be home to a vast array of exotic fish. Its location on the edge of the American continental shelf and proximity to the Gulf Stream made it a paradise for marine researchers. Within a few minutes travel, scientists could be astride a coral reef or in waters that dropped to astonishing depths. In addition to an incredibly diverse marine biology, the nearby shallow waters of the Bahama Bank were crystal clear, allowing for unfettered observation of marine life in its natural habitat. All this was abundantly clear to Gregory and he wasted no time in signaling his enthusiasm for the project.

Lerner soon purchased the land and construction of the new facility was underway. However, when word of the project leaked to the scientific community, the subsequent clamor resulted in a dramatic enlargement over what had been originally conceived. By the time everything was completed in 1948, the sparkling facility could accommodate up to 12 scientists at a time with all of their daily needs provided by Lerner. Scientists wishing to work at the lab would petition a Museum-appointed advisory committee, and the waiting list quickly grew to more than 150 applicants. The Lerner Marine Laboratory was an exceptional gesture of selflessness on Lerner's part and one that would provide him with lifelong stimulation and satisfaction.

In addition to a complete laboratory, the facility included a darkroom, dissecting facilities, a specimen pool with more than 1,500 living examples of marine life open to public view, and one of the first closed-circuit TV connections hooked to an underwater camera offshore. Residents and guests alike would spend hours staring in mesmerized silence at the live underwater world nearby. Early scientific projects included studies in fish taxonomy,[14] sponge chemistry, and Gulf Stream observations and experimentation. While attempts at penning live white marlin and sailfish proved unsuccessful, the Lab's early success with maintaining dolphin in captivity would later give rise to aquatic parks such as Marineland and Sea World. Subsequent efforts gravitated towards cancer research, as funding was generous for such work and fish had a surprising number of characteristics useful in oncology studies.[15] Admission to the facility was always free, and countless visitors to the island would emerge from the Lerner Lab as ardent supporters. Eternally dedicated, Lerner would participate actively in the Lab until its closure in the early 1970s.

A dolphin performs on cue for guests at the Lerner Marine Laboratory.

Perhaps the most celebrated big-game angler of all time, Mike Lerner nevertheless was eternally modest about his achievements with rod and reel. Among other accomplishments, he captured 23 swordfish in his angling career during a time when big-game fishing tackle, techniques, and boats were in their most primitive states. Remarkably, he took two swordfish in one day on four separate occasions, two black marlin in one day off Australia (an unprecedented achievement at the time) and many other angling firsts. Widely recognized by many nations for his contributions to both angling and science, his aid in establishing a sportfishing industry in Europe after WWII helped raise the standard of living for many Basque subsistence fishermen. In 1978, Michael Lerner died at his home in Miami at age 86, a contented man of many gifts.

55

All this, and the IGFA too.

---

[14] *For example, fish locomotion.*

[15] *Fish are prone to tumors, less biologically complicated, relatively easy to control and study, and available (at least in Bimini) in great quantity, quality and at nominal cost.*

A contented Mike Lerner at his beloved laboratory.

An early view of the American Museum of Natural History in New York, home to the IGFA during its formative years.

Chapter Three

GETTING STARTED

Despite the news from overseas, Lerner must have felt a thrill of anticipation as the International Game Fish Association opened for business. With staffing and finances already in place as a result of its inaugural meeting, the IGFA then had to decide what to do. The needs were legion: create a portfolio of standardized angling rules along with a rigorous ethical credo, assume the responsibility of saltwater record-keeping from *Field & Stream,* develop a network of International Representatives to promulgate IGFA principles in distant lands and, not least, find a place to work. This last need was generously met by the American Museum of Natural History when it agreed to house the new organization in Museum offices. Such an offer was not made lightly, as Museum office space was in chronically short supply and various other groups

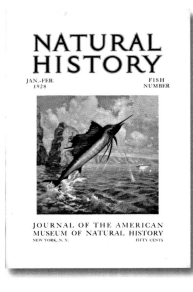

NATURAL HISTORY

JAN.-FEB. 1928   FISH NUMBER

JOURNAL OF THE AMERICAN
MUSEUM OF NATURAL HISTORY
NEW YORK, N. Y.   FIFTY CENTS

were always lobbying for Museum sponsorship and support. Nevertheless, Michael Lerner's enormous contributions to the AMNH could not be overlooked, and it was just good business for the Museum to keep its best patrons happy. Besides, maybe the new group would eventually make something of itself.

Surely a more disparate-looking bunch could hardly be found. At front and center was Lerner: world-class outdoorsman and angler, hugely successful entrepreneur, a stocky and robust man with a bashful smile and engaging manner. Next to Lerner was Dr. William K. Gregory, senior ichthyologist at the Museum and perhaps the most widely-celebrated scientist in his field. His avuncular face, ever-present spectacles, and sterling academic credentials granted the fledgling group instant credibility, and he was promptly elected to serve as the IGFA's first President. Next to him was Francesca LaMonte, a most capable staff scientist at the Museum who would later prove herself totally dedicated to Lerner and his ideals. Quiet and reserved, LaMonte would serve the IGFA for nearly 40 years. Finally, there was Van Campen Heilner, patrician author and playboy with an insatiable love of the sea. Good-looking and youthful, his own fishing exploits were already vast and he quickly became a tireless promoter and master of organizational detail. As he looked around the crowded office at his army of three, Lerner could hardly know that his little group would accomplish so much.

Dr. William K. Gregory, esteemed ichthyologist and the IGFA's first President.

Van Campen Heilner, author and sportsman.

As the organization got underway, its early emphasis was on gathering data for marine scientists and providing a worldwide view of angling opportunities and conditions. World War II was a substantial impediment to that second goal, but beginning in 1941 the IGFA published three scientific "white papers" under its own imprint that attempted to clarify questions relating to game fish species.[1] This output plus the ongoing AMNH affiliation gave the IGFA a tremendous boost of initial credibility. Word began to spread of the new goings-on in New York, and both visitors and correspondence increased dramatically. In short order, the IGFA outgrew its allotted space and was relocated to larger offices within the Museum's charming Department of Herpetology.

Despite the obstacles presented by the war, the IGFA also moved ahead with putting in place an International Committee that could deliver a global overview of angling activities. Within six months, the IGFA had 12 overseas Representatives,[2] a number that would more than double during the difficult war years. The formation of an International Committee was (and remains) a cornerstone of IGFA strategy: Representatives functioned as resources for local anglers and also served as conduits back to New York for regional angling conditions. Indeed, so outward-looking was the original focus that the USA itself had no direct representation on the International Committee until the post of IGFA Associate was created in 1949.[3] Interestingly, no other similar organization before or since has been as successful with this concept,[4] and over the years many different groups have expressed their admiration and envy of same. If nothing else, the IGFA founders would discover through their Representatives where to go for their next angling adventure.

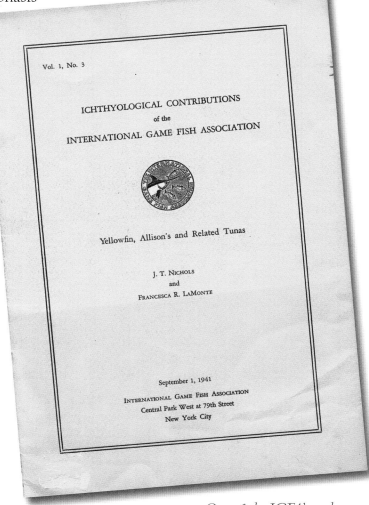

One of the IGFA's early "white papers," this one dated September of 1941.

[1] Not all were particularly rigorous: paper No. 3 shown above sought to identify several non-existent species of yellowfin tuna.

[2] Including Clive Firth in Australia and a young Lee Wulff in Newfoundland.

[3] Associate appointees included Miami Herald columnist Erl Roman and former Tuna Club President Joe Peeler before the position was abolished in favor of regional Representatives.

[4] In 2004, the IGFA's International Committee included 330 Representatives in 100 countries.

The IGFA's organizational structure also allowed for affiliations with other institutions and clubs, and within a year there were two member scientific institutions and 10 member clubs.[5] Early on, Lerner shrewdly recognized that the organization would attract little notice unless a network of credible relationships was already in place. Work on creating these affiliations had begun right away, and the IGFA's first year was spent almost entirely dedicated to this task. As a result, the IGFA kept a low profile during its first 18 months, waiting until everything was ready before publicly proclaiming its existence. When the time came to do so, the IGFA could boast of such esteemed scientific members as the Smithsonian Institution and the British Museum of Natural History. Two years later (1943), the list of scientific affiliations was at six and the number of member clubs stood at 27, a sterling start in the midst of world war.

---

[5]*The first being the Cape Breton Big Game Anglers Association in Louisburg, Nova Scotia.*

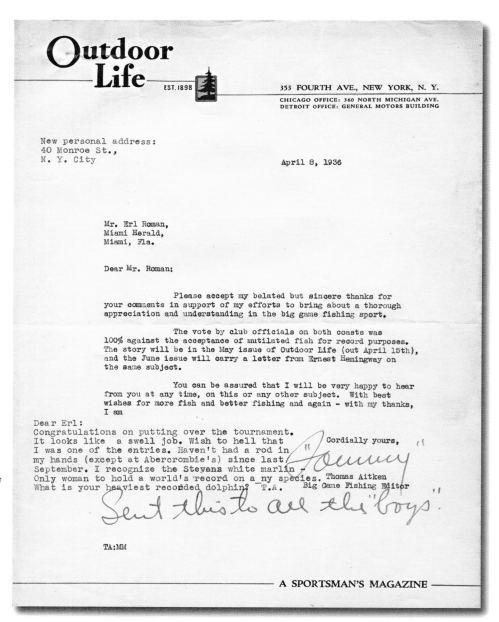

Early outdoor writers Tommy Aitken and Erl Roman were frequent correspondents about newsworthy events in the world of angling. Both went on to play key roles in helping to promote the IGFA.

61

Throughout his business career, Lerner always had a remarkably keen understanding of the press, and it served him well in launching the IGFA. Florida outdoor writers Tommy Aitken and Erl Roman had long been lobbying for such an association: Aitken through his affiliation with *Outdoor Life* magazine and Roman as Big Game Fishing Editor for the *Miami Herald*. Aitken in particular had been beating the organizational drum since the mid-1930s, writing many letters and maintaining a lengthy correspondence with Clive Firth. He had even proposed several names for such a body, including the Sea Angling Society and Marine Wildlife Association.[6] On these and other matters, Lerner carefully cultivated both Aitken and Roman, and both writers were primed when the IGFA was finally ready to launch. Once underway, Lerner reciprocated by using the pair to disseminate early IGFA press releases and world record information. As it happened, the IGFA had no mechanism for typing and distributing 300 press releases anyway, so the arrangement proved ideal for all parties.

---

[6]*However, Francesca LaMonte appears to be the first to suggest the International Game Fish Association name in a letter to Lerner dated July 3, 1939. She felt that such a name would be more unique, sufficiently descriptive, and less reminiscent of a governmental organization.*

During this early period, Lerner worked tirelessly to build a foundation of broad support. He knew the British Tunny Club was unhappy that its own proposal to serve as the sport's governing body hadn't been received more kindly, but Lerner's argument for an altogether new organization with scientific sponsorship was hard to ignore. Still miffed, the British Tunny Club refused to participate in the original planning for the IGFA, prompting a series of letters from Lerner and Heilner that attempted to smooth things over. The British finally came around and by war's end counted themselves as firm supporters. Lerner also tapped his media connections and the likes of tackle baron Julian Crandall for their mailing lists, and he sent scores of personally composed letters to fishing clubs around the world. As a result, the list of member clubs grew steadily.

Nevertheless, not all clubs were initially welcome. In keeping with the IGFA's amateur status, clubs consisting of professional guides or boatmen were excluded from early membership. Not surprisingly, this proved to be a point of contention with such clubs as the Tuna Guides Association of Wedgeport, a group that Lerner was largely responsible for creating. However, IGFA secretary Francesca LaMonte held firm in her communications back to the Wedgeport group that all IGFA member clubs must be non-commercial and non-professional. There were to be no exceptions. The Tuna Guides Association reluctantly conceded, but several new clubs were spawned under different guidelines just so that they might become members of the IGFA.

With gamefish study and international data-gathering efforts underway, the IGFA turned its attention to angling ethics and rules. Lerner was adamant that the IGFA remain an amateur organization with no dues, no political affiliations, and no commercial endorsements. He even went so far as to insist that IGFA officers shouldn't be allowed to hold world records lest their judgment be clouded when evaluating a superior catch. IGFA officers should be above reproach, Lerner maintained, and the other officers unanimously concurred. Nevertheless, the IGFA's motto "For Ethical Sport and Productive Science" was carefully crafted in such a way as to recognize that science and sport were not mutually exclusive. Both could be pursued in ways that aided the other, and if science occasionally required the taking of marine specimens in a not-very-sportsmanlike manner, that was OK, too. With such a flexible framework in place, the work then turned to the crafting of rules.

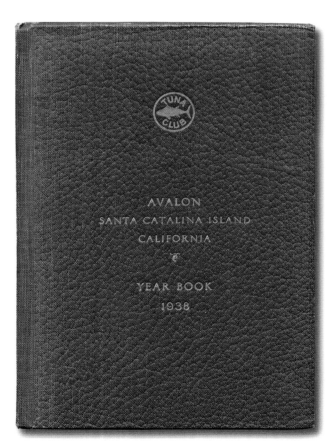

Tuna Club angling rules provided a helpful foundation but were a bit too exacting for IGFA rule-makers.

Outdoor Life
EST. 1898

353 FOURTH AVE., NEW YORK, N. Y.

CHICAGO OFFICE: 360 NORTH MICHIGAN AVE.
DETROIT OFFICE: GENERAL MOTORS BUILDING

April 27, 1936

Mr. Erl Roman,
Miami Herald,
Miami, Fla.

Dear Erl:

  The enclosed blanks are for use in recording outstanding catches. They are self explanatory. When you
want more of them let me know. If I hear of anyone catching a big fish in your waters they will be instructec to
get a blank from you. Thanks for your cooperation.

        Cordially yours,

        Thomas Aitken
        Thomas Aitken
        Big Game Fishing Editor

TA:MM

*Aitken's own efforts at
record-keeping on behalf
of Outdoor Life were
deliberate and well-organized.
His records were ultimately
blended with those of Field
& Stream to create the
IGFA's first world record list.*

Outdoor Life
A SPORTSMAN'S MAGAZINE

O F F I C I A L   R E C O G N I T I O N
(This blank to be used in recording outstanding salt water game fish catches)

SPECIES ....
WEIGHT ....Length ....Date Caught ....
TIME REQUIRED ....Girth ....Tail Span ....
Make of Rod ....Waters Where Caught ....Weight of Tip ....Reel Make ....
Make of Line ....Size ....Lure or bait used ....Size ....
Name of Angler (Print) ....
State Temporary Address ....
Permanent Address ....
Are you an angling club member?(If so, state club) ....
Name of Guide ....
Name of Boat ....Address ....
Was Fish Mutilated? ....Home Port ....
........................(If so, state how it happened)

Was this fish brought to gaff without assistance under recognized ethics and rules as con-
strued by representative angling clubs? (Yes or No) ....
Witnesses of weight and measurements:
Name ....
Name ....Address ....
........................Address ....
Species identified as such by the following competent authority:
Name ....
........................Address ....
(Marlin and tuna must be positively identified by their sub species name or color)

Either affidavit or verification by official of representative angling club must accompany
this recognition blank if a record claim is made. If possible a clear photograph of fish
should also accompany claim, such photograph to become the property of OUTDOOR LIFE.
I hereby swear that all statements contained herein are true.
SIGNATURE OF ANGLER ....
Sworn to before me this ....day of .... 193....
Notary signature and seal

Recognition is given to heaviest salt water game fish of all species caught by both men and
women anglers in the following classifications: WORLD'S RECORDS - PACIFIC RECORDS -
ATLANTIC RECORDS - NORTH AMERICAN RECORDS - UNITED STATES COASTAL RECORDS
Forward to:
THOMAS AITKEN, Big Game Fishing Editor, OUTDOOR LIFE, 353 Fourth Avenue, New York, N. Y.

After much deliberation by the attendant parties, it was decided that angling rules should emphasize line class as the most important variable. Other factors associated with angling tackle (e.g., rod length, reel diameter) were regarded as of secondary importance. Line must be made entirely of 50-lea linen yarn, and the number of threads used in the line's construction would define the line class. The IGFA's first rules delineated six different line classes in which world record consideration would be granted: 6-thread, 9-thread, 15-thread, 24-thread, 39-thread, and 54-thread. With each thread delivering approximately three pounds of breaking strength, this meant that 6-thread line would break at some 18 pounds of pressure, 9-thread at 27 pounds pressure, and so forth. Catches made on line with in-between thread counts (e.g., 12-thread) would be considered within the next highest line class (15-thread).

Other tackle requirements were largely based on those of the Tuna Club of Catalina Island. Nevertheless, some concessions were necessary due to the ultra-conservative approach embodied by Tuna Club rules. For example, the Tuna Club did not recognize line classes in excess of 24-thread, but certain regions of the world commonly utilized such heavier lines in their local fisheries.[7] Knowing that, and in an effort to show some latitude, the IGFA broadened the allowable line selection to be as inclusive as possible. Similarly, while the IGFA's new rules were specific in regulating the use of leader and

---

[7]*To this day, Tuna Club rules remain the most restrictive in the world. Indeed, IGFA archives include a prickly unsigned letter sent to the Tuna Club excoriating them for adhering to obsolete angling rules.*

Early linen line was wound on wooden spools and sold by thread count.

Philip Wylie

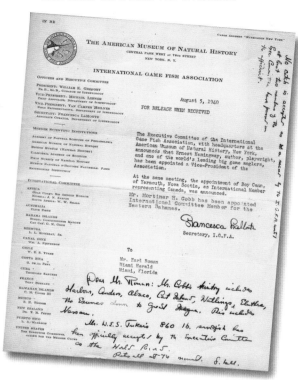

In August of 1940, this press release announced that Ernest Hemingway had been made an IGFA Vice President.

double line, rods of virtually any sort could be used so long as the angler was not provided of an unsportsmanlike advantage. From the beginning, the IGFA set exceedingly high angling standards, but not unreasonably or arbitrarily so. In Lerner's view, anyone who followed a few rules and accepted the basic tenants of sportsmanship was worthy of holding an IGFA world record.

As the organization struggled to its feet during the war years, the IGFA made several critical changes to its senior staff. In 1940, Ernest Hemingway came aboard as Vice President and the following year Philip Wylie was elected to the newly-created post of Field Representative. Both men were avid anglers and exceedingly talented writers, and both were in complete agreement with the high ethical standards that the IGFA was trying to establish. While Hemingway would contribute relatively little during his 21 years of association, Wylie proved to be a whirlwind of activity. Tall, lean, dour, with a chronically slumping posture, Wylie wrote thousands of words in support of the IGFA during his long tenure. As with Hemingway, his brand of writing was distinctive and unique. It sparkled with enthusiasm and imaginative descriptions, and no reader could doubt the writer's sincere interest in his subject. Wylie was vehement in making his point, underlining key phrases and unafraid of inventing a new word to suit the occasion. Next to Lerner, he was the hardest working of the original IGFA angler/founders.

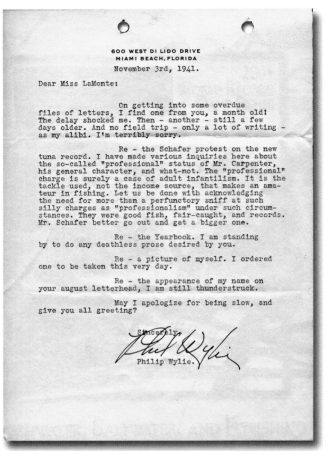

600 WEST DI LIDO DRIVE
MIAMI BEACH, FLORIDA
November 3rd, 1941.

Dear Miss LaMonte:

On getting into some overdue files of letters, I find one from you, a month old! The delay shocked me. Then - another - still a few days older. And no field trip - only a lot of writing - as my alibi. I'm terribly sorry.

Re - the Schafer protest on the new tuna record. I have made various inquiries here about the so-called "professional" status of Mr. Carpenter, his general character, and what-not. The "professional" charge is surely a case of adult infantilism. It is the tackle used, not the income source, that makes an amateur in fishing. Let us be done with acknowledging the need for more than a perfunctory sniff at such silly charges as "professionalism" under such circumstances. They were good fish, fair-caught, and records. Mr. Schafer better go out and get a bigger one.

Re - the Yearbook. I am standing by to do any deathless prose desired by you.

Re - a picture of myself. I ordered one to be taken this very day.

Re - the appearance of my name on your august letterhead, I am still thunderstruck.

May I apologize for being slow, and give you all greeting?

Sincerely,

Philip Wylie.

Philip Wylie and Mike Lerner in Bimini at the opening of the Lerner Marine Laboratory (1948).

Even mundane letters like this one from Wylie to Francesca LaMonte were artfully worded.

66

In 1944, Gregory retired from the AMNH and concurrently stepped down from his role as President of the IGFA. Gregory knew little of angling and was originally put in place largely as a gesture to the Museum. Nevertheless, his initial enthusiasm was instrumental in fueling Lerner's own, and he contributed much to the early ichthyological goals of the organization. Long-faced and professorial, Gregory was very much the academic but proved to be most approachable and a perfect choice as the IGFA's first President. Not surprisingly, Michael Lerner was unanimously installed as IGFA's next President, and his service over the next 16 years would set the bar very high indeed for his successors.

By war's end in 1945, the IGFA had completed its organizational thinking and released a small publication detailing its goals and accomplishments to date. The organization's four-fold stated mission was now in print:

1. To encourage the study of game fishes for whatever purpose;
2. To set and maintain the highest standards of ethics and create rules accordingly;
3. To encourage recreational angling and data accumulation surrounding same; and
4. To maintain a listing of world record catches.

Clearly, the IGFA was to serve science as well as sport, and Gregory's status as President Emeritus was a strong reinforcement of that message.[8] The IGFA now had three Vice Presidents, having elevated Wylie to the same rank as Heilner and Hemingway. The International Committee was up to 28 members, scientific affiliates now numbered eight, and there were 37 member angling clubs throughout the known world...not bad from a standing start just a few war-torn years before.

For the first time, this new 1945 publication also carefully documented IGFA procedures for evaluating world record catches. In case of an identity dispute, professional ichthyologists (presumably from the Museum) would decide the outcome.

---

[8] *The AMNH maintained its influence with the appointment of Dr. Charles M. Breder Jr. as the IGFA's Chairman on Scientific Activities. Breder was the incoming Curator of the AMNH's Department of Fishes.*

67

THE INTERNATIONAL GAME FISH ASSOCIATION
(For Ethical Sport and Productive Science)

ORGANIZATION

and

RULES

International Game Fish Association
The American Museum of Natural History
New York 24, New York

U.S.A.

The IGFA's first organizational booklet published in 1945.

All submissions for world record consideration must now include a certified weight slip, length and girth measurements of the catch, photos (where possible) and affidavits from all participants. In order to capitalize on fresh recollections and eliminate the wistful submission of old catches, a time limit of 60 days for domestic captures and 90 days for international catches was instituted. Applications made past that time period would not be considered, and a number of other specific actions were also identified as being disqualifying events. For the first time, exactitude and rigor were reflected in the rules, and serious anglers worldwide were decidedly pleased.

By war's end, each of the IGFA's founding officers had settled into their respective roles. Lerner was the financier, strategist, and world face of the IGFA; his reputation was impeccable and his personal ethics known to be of the highest sort. Wylie was a workhorse, churning out articles and promotional pieces on behalf of the organization when he wasn't penning books, screenplays, and his lyrical "Crunch and Des" articles for the *Saturday Evening Post*.[9] Although the least accomplished angler among the IGFA sportsmen, his contributions were immense and he was later designated a First Vice President, the only one ever so named. As Secretary, Francesca LaMonte

[9]The Post *published 49 "Crunch and Des" stories from 1939-1956, and some 20 others appeared elsewhere.*

Wylie's "Crunch and Des" stories were later combined into best-selling anthologies that still make great reading today.

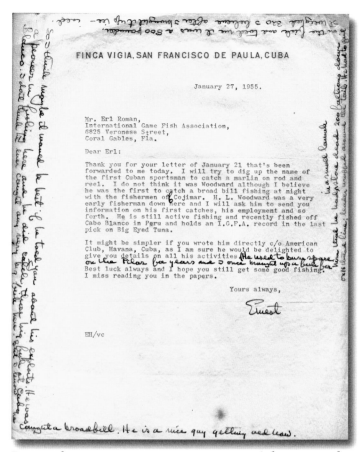

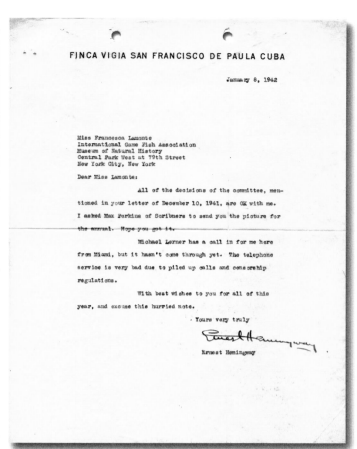

Despite their frequent messiness, Hemingway's letters regarding IGFA business were both helpful and warm.

handled all day-to-day responsibilities, dealing with inquiries, visitors, correspondence, record submissions and a host of other details. Her early assistant[10] recalls that she spent most of her day on IGFA business and relatively
little on AMNH matters, but her co-authorship over the years of several
books on fish identification was evidently enough to satisfy the Museum.

Of the IGFA's two other officers, little can be said of Ernest Hemingway
that hasn't been said before. His contributions to the organization were
mostly in the form of internal commentary and the occasional article in
support of angling ethics. More notably, Hemingway was a frequent guest
of the Lerners at their sprawling Bimini complex and doubtlessly helped
Lerner work through his original ideas on what the IGFA should do. Despite
a legendary reputation for recklessness, he was also extremely high-minded in
his approach to the sporting life. Fishing was religion to Hemingway, and he
would deliberate with great care as to which element of tackle would create
the most meaningful sporting experience. As a result, he and Lerner saw eye-
to-eye when it came to applying a high ethical standard to the pursuit of big
game.

---

[10]*Eula Jorgensen, interviewed by phone on August 16, 2004.*

WORLD'S RECORD FISH

Catches With Rod and Reel and Otherwise of Popular North American Fresh- and Salt-Water Fish

Revised to 1928

Compiled by John Treadwell Nichols of the American Museum of Natural History and Van Campen Heilner of FIELD AND STREAM

The following list, which is a valuable addition to both the sporting and scientific world, was compiled by the authors only after months of painstaking research and unceasing labor.—Ed.

For a subject of such general interest, it is surprising how little information is available on the record size of fish. It is with this in mind that we have gathered the information set forth in the accompanying table.

In some cases it was impossible to secure circumstantial data concerning fish of maximum size for their species, and we have been obliged to quote general statements which, to the best of our belief, are correct. We have taken such from four well-recognized authorities: U. S. Bureau of Fisheries, Jordan and Evermann, G. Brown Goode, and FIELD AND STREAM's Prize Fishing Contest. Estimates of weight or length are in most cases based on mathematical calculations.

The record fish lists published in the past met with such approval that the authors have been much encouraged in the preparation of this one. The only way in which it can be perfected for the future is by expression of opinion. If anyone has suggestions or knows of fish which exceed in size the ones mentioned, kindly send us full details, which we will be only too happy to receive.

FRESH-WATER FISH

SPECIES	Scientific Name	Greatest Weight Rod and Reel	Length	Girth	Where Caught	Date Caught	By Whom Caught	Greatest Wt. Caught by Any Method	Length	Girth	Where Caught	Date Caught	By Whom Caught
Black Bass (Large-mouth)	Micropterus salmoides	24 lbs.	Approx. 35"	24"	Tombigbee R. Ala.	April 11 1926	George J. Nicholls	Same	...	...	......	......	......
Black Bass (Small-mouth)	Micropterus dolomieu	9¼ lbs.	Approx. 27¼"	Est. 16½"	Long Lake, Aloha Twp., Cheboygan Co. Mich.	Aug. 1926	Wm. F. Shoemaker	Same	...	...	......	......	......
Carp	Cyprinus carpio	23 lbs.	...	...	Wickham Lake, N. Y.	Sept. 9 1924	John C. Lawrence	90 lbs.	...	...	Lake of Zug, Switzerland	About 1825	......
Catfish (Mississippi)	Ameiurus lacustris	......	...	...	......	...	.....	150 lbs.	5'	...	St. Louis, Mo.	About 1878	Rep. by U.S. Nat. Mus.
Gar (Alligator)	Lepisosteus ferox	......	...	...	......	...	.....	.....	12'	...	Sulphur, La.	.....	Killed with axe by M'sieu Tata Ibert
Muskalonge	Esox masquinongy	51 lbs. 3 oz.	54"	26½"	Lake Vieux, Desert, Wis.	July 16 1919	J. A. Knobla	Over 75 lbs.	...	...	Minocqua Lake, Wis.	May 1 1906	Wisconsin Fish & Game Commission
Pike (Northern)	Esox estor	36 lbs. 8 oz.	50¼"	21¼"	Clearwater Lake, Ont.	Aug. 28 1925	Wm. E. Bostwick	Same	...	...	......	.....	......
Pike (Wall-eyed)	Stizostedion vitreum	17 lbs.	35½"	29"	White River, Indiana	April 9 1919	Aaron Abel	40 lbs.	...	...		.....	Rep. by U.S. Fish Commission
Perch (Yellow)	Perca flavescens	4 lbs. 3½ oz.	Est. 16"	...	Bordentown, N. J.	May 1865	Dr. C. C. Abbot	Same	...	...			
Salmon (Atlantic)	Salmo salar	69½ lbs.	...	...	Aaro R. Norway	1921	Johann Aarven	83 lbs.	...	...	Great Britain	1821	Rep. by Goode in "Amer. Fishes"
Salmon (Chinook)	Oncorhynchus tschawytscha	70 lbs.	...	...	Campbell R. Vancouver I. B. C.	Sept. 1897	Sir Richard Musgrave	Over 100 lbs.	...	...	Yukon River, Alaska	.....	Rep. by U.S. Fish Commission
Sturgeon (American)	Acipenser	......	...	...	......	...	.....	1000 lbs.	10' 5"	...	Columbia R. Oregon	Opening Day of Season 1911	Clyde Leiser
Trout (Brook)	Salvelinus fontinalis	14½ lbs.	...	...	Nipigon R. Ont. Canada	July 1916	Dr. W. J. Cook	Same	...	...			
Trout (Rainbow)	Salmo irideus	26½ lbs.	42"	27"	Skycomish River, Wash.	July 12 1914	A. A. Cass	Same	...	...			......
Trout (Lake)	Christivomer namaycush	42 lbs. 8 oz.	44"	29"	Isle Royale, Mich.	July 16 1924	Elling A. Seglem	80 lbs.	...	...	Mackinaw Mich.	Abt. 1878	Rep. by U.S. Nat'l Museum
Trout (Steelhead)	Salmo truncatus	22 lbs.	39"	17"	E. Lake, Bend, Ore.	June 5 1920	Homer Marsh	42 lbs.	...	...	Corbett, Col. R. Oregon	1903	Reed Bros.— U. S. Bur. Fisheries
Trout (Cut-throat)	Salmo clarkii	41 lbs.	39"	...	Pyramid Lake, Nixon, Nev.	Dec. 1925	John Skimmerhorn	Same	...	...	......	.....	......
Trout (Brown)	Salmo eriox	25 lbs. 5¼ oz.	37½"	22½"	Logan R. Utah	July 17 1924	W. W. Smart	28½ lbs.	...	...	New Zealand	.....	Exhibited at World's Fair, St.Louis—1904.

*For the following rod and reel records the authors are indebted to the *Field and Stream* Prize Fishing Contest: muskalonge, great northern pike, rainbow trout, lake trout, steelhead trout, cut-throat trout, striped bass, channel bass, weakfish.

Copyright, 1928, by Van Campen Heilner and J. T. Nichols

Early world record charts compiled by Heilner and John T. Nichols of the AMNH (1928). Such charts were published annually in Field & Stream *and distributed in large poster form to marinas, tackle shops, and angling clubs.*

SALT-WATER FISH

SPECIES	Scientific Name	Greatest Weight Rod and Reel	Length	Girth	Where Caught	Date Caught	By Whom Caught	Greatest Wt. Caught by Any Method	Length	Girth	Where Caught	Date Caught	By Whom Caught
Amberjack	Seriola lalandi	95 lbs.	...	...	Long Key, Florida	1916	S. W. Eccles	134 lbs.	7'	...	St. George Bermuda	Jan. 1928	Thos. Bartram
Albacore	Germo alalunga	66 lbs. 4 oz.	...	...	Santa Catalina Isl., Cal.	1912	Frank Kelly	Same	...	...	.....	.....	.....
Bass (Striped)	Roccus lineatus	73 lbs.	60"	30½"	Vineyard Sound, Mass.	Aug. 17 1913	Chas. B. Church	125 lbs.	...	...	Edenton, No. Carolina	April 1891	Netted by fishermen
Bass (Channel)	Sciaenops ocellatus	65 lbs.	49"	35"	New Inlet, N. J.	Sept. 24 1919	Chas. H. Smith	75 lbs.	5'	...	.....	.....	Reported by Jordan & Evermann
Bass (Cal. Black Sea)	Stereolepis gigas	515 lbs.	...	...	Santa Catalina Isl., Cal.	1916	Wallace Beerley	800 lbs.	...	...	Avalon, Cal.	1902	......
Bass (Cal. White Sea)	Cynoscion nobilis	60 lbs.	...	...	Santa Catalina Isl., Cal.	May 23 1904	C. H. Harding	Same	...	...	.....	.....	......
Bass (Sea)	Centropristes striatus	8 lbs. 2 oz.	...	...	Banks off New York	...	Peter Volkman	Same	...	...	.....	.....	
Barracuda (Great)	Sphyraena barracuda	64 lbs. 4 oz.	...	...	Off Miami, Fla.	April 18 1924	A. H. Peterson	.....	Over 10'	...	Bahamas	.....	Non-authenticated report
Bluefish	Pomatomus saltatrix	25 lbs.	Est. 42"	...	Cohasset Narrows, Mass.	June 16 1874	L. Hathaway	27 lbs.	45"	...	Maddequet Life S. S. Nantucket, Mass.	Sept. 1903	Nelson P. Emer
Bonefish	Albula vulpes	13¾ lbs.	31"	17"	Isl. of Bimini, Bahamas	Mar. 9 1919	B. F. Peek	Same	...	...	.....	.....	In collection Amer. Mus. Nat. History
Cero (or Fla. Kingfish)	Scomberomorus cavalla	58 lbs.	...	...	Long Key, Florida	April 1927	Mae Haines	100 lbs.	...	...	.....	.....	Reported by Jordan & Evermann
Codfish	Gadus callarias	52 lbs.	...	...	Banks off New York	...	Fred Foster, also Pat Regan	211½ lbs.	Over 6'	...	Off Mass.	May 1895	Market Fishermen
Drum (Black)	Pogonias cromis	90 lbs.	...	...	Surf City, N. J.	June 21 1925	Capt. Jack Inman	146 lbs.	...	...	St. Augustine, Fla.	.....	Reported by Jordan & Everman
Dolphin	Coryphaena hippurus	51½ lbs.	...	...	Galapagos Islands	Feb. 1925	Zane Grey	.....	6'	...	High Seas	.....	Reported by Jordan & Evermann
Flounder (Summer)	Paralichthys dentatus	19 lbs.	...	...	Banks off N. Y. from "Seth Low"	About 1895	Fred Foster	26 lbs.	Est. 46"	...	Noank, Conn.	June	Reported in "Amer. Fishes"—Goode
Halibut	Hippoglossus hippoglossus	......	...	...	......	...	.....	Dressed 625 lbs.	9' 2"	Br'dth 4' 6"	50 miles N. of Thatcher's Isl., Mass.	June 1917	Capt. A. S. Ree in "Eva Avina"
Jewfish	Promicrops guttatus	542 lbs.	...	...	Sarasota, Florida	May 1923	W. E. Lincoln	693 lbs.	96"	76"	Caesar's Creek, Fla.	Jan. 22 1923	Dr. J. Lawn Thompson
Manta (or Devilfish)	Manta birostris	......	...	...	......	...	.....	Over 3000 lbs.	17' 2"	Width 22	Island of Bimini, Bahamas	Feb. 14 1919	Harpooned by Chas. Thompson
Mola (or Ocean Sunfish)	Mola mola	......	...	...	......	...	.....	Est. over 2000 lbs.	10' 11"	Br'dth 10' 9"	Santa Catalina Isl. Cal.	Sept. 3 1919	Harpooned by Van Campen Heilner
Ray (Whip)	Aetobatus narinari	......	...	...	......	...	.....	Est. 450 lbs.	12'	Width 7' 7"	Cape Lookout, N. C.	July 1912	Harpooned by Russel J. Coles
Swordfish (Striped Marlin)	Makaira mitsikurii	450 lbs.	11' 5"	4' 2"	New Zealand	March 1926	Zane Grey	780 lbs.	...	...	Hawaiian Isls.	.....	Rep. by David Starr Jordan
Swordfish (Black Marlin)	Makaira marlina	976 lbs.	12' 8"	6' 2"	New Zealand	Jan. 1926	L. D. Mitchell	1080 lbs.	10' without sword	...	Misaki, Japan	May 1901	Seen in fish market by Dr. Jordan
Swordfish (Broadbill)	Xiphias gladius	588 lbs.	13' 1"	5' 6"	Santa Catalina Isl., Cal.	July 28 1927	R. C. Grey	Est. 1000 lbs.	...	...	New England	.....	Capt. Hillman
Sailfish (Pacific)	Istiophorus greyi	160 lbs.	10' 10"	...	Gulf of Lower Cal., Mex.	Nov. 1925	L. I. Hollingsworth	177½ lbs.	10' 4"	...	Pearl Ids. Bay of Panama	June 23, 1927	C. F. Underhill W. H. Keenan H. H. Hammer
Sawfish	Pristis pectinatus	600 lbs.	14'	Br'dth 54"	Ft. Myers, Fla.	May 2 1897	E. Vom Hofe	.....	17' 8"	...	Cape Sable, Fla.	Mar. 1918	Harpooned by Van Campen Heilner
Shark (Whale)	Rhineodon typus	......	...	...	......	...	.....	Est. 26,594 lbs.	38'	18'	Knight's Key, Fla.	June 1 1912	Harpooned by Chas. Thompson
Shark (Mako)	Isurus	2176 lbs.	13' 3"	8' 9"	Hermanus, Cape, Province, So. Africa	June 1928	W. R. Selkirk	Same	...	...	.....	.....	......
Tuna	Thunnus thynnus	758 lbs.	8' 8"	6' 4"	Port Medway, Nova Scotia	Aug. 22 1924	Zane Grey	1500 lbs.	...	...	.....	.....	Rep. by Jordan & Evermann
Tarpon	Tarpon atlanticus	232 lbs.	7' 8"	47"	Panuco River, Mexico	March 1911	W. A. McLaren	Est. 350 lbs.	8' 2"	...	Hillsboro R. Inlet, Fla.	Aug. 6 1912	Netted by native Fishermen
Tautog (or Blackfish)	Tautoga onitis	20 lbs. 4 oz.	...	...	Banks off N. Y. from "Schuyler"	...	Lewis Harm	22½ lbs.	36¼"	...	Near New York	July 1876	In collection of U. S. Nat'l Museum, Wash. D. C.
Wahoo	Acanthocybium solandri	86 lbs.	75"	...	Nassau, Bahamas	Mar. 1911	Wm. E. Carlin	100 lbs.	6'	...	West Indies	.....	Rep. by Jordan & Evermann
Weakfish	Cynoscion regalis	16 lbs. 8 oz.	36"	19"	Fire Island Inlet, N. Y.	Oct. 15 1924	John D. Wolf	30 lbs.	...	...	New Jersey	.....	Rep. by Goode in "Amer. Fishes"
Yellowtail (Cal.)	Seriola dorsalis	111 lbs.	...	...	New Zealand	1926	Zane Grey	Same	...	...	.....	...	

In contrast, much less has been written about IGFA founding Vice President Van Campen Heilner. A child of privilege, Heilner was a distinct opposite of Hemingway in appearance. His aristocratic features, blond hair, blue eyes, and classically handsome countenance could have opened many doors, but few men in history have shown as much dedication to the sport of angling as did Heilner. Born August 1, 1899 into a wealthy mining family,[11] Van Campen Heilner was blessed in triplicate with looks, money, and brains. His father was an avid lover of the outdoors and encouraged his son's interest at an early age. Heilner studied at Phillips Academy (Andover, Massachusetts) and the Lake Placid (Florida) School, both established stopping-off points for the well-to-do. Nevertheless, Heilner showed little interest in the family firm, preferring instead to spend every possible moment on the water with rod in hand. Summers on the Jersey shore furthered his enthusiasm for angling, and a family holiday in Bimini resulted in his meeting legendary angler and author Zane Grey. Grey's writing success and wanderlust sounded like the perfect life to Heilner, and he spent the rest of his days in pursuit of that ideal.

---

[11] *The family firm was Percy Heilner & Son, established 1854, with offices throughout the northeastern U.S.*

A young Heilner visits with Zane Grey on Long Key (1916).

Unlike Grey, Heilner was prolific at an early age and saw a number of his boating and fishing articles published before his twentieth birthday. At 21, he co-wrote[12] his first book on surf fishing, and two years later he authored *Adventures in Angling*, an incredibly diverse work for a young man of just 23 years. The book was a compendium of his angling experiences spanning both coasts, and in it he documented his battles with marlin, sailfish, salmon, tarpon, tuna, and many other species. Heilner wrote passionately of his enthusiasm for light tackle ("the ONLY tackle" as he described it) and was ardent in his support of conservation.[13] *Adventures in Angling* also included a 1916 map of southwest Florida drawn by W. P. Patterson, one of the first modern sketches of this previously little-known area. The book was a triumph, and Heilner was a made man.

Heilner's certificate from the Tuna Club that accompanied his button (1921).

In 1920, he visited Bimini again and decided to establish a seasonal camp there, becoming the first white resident among the native islanders. Already predisposed towards the island's beauty, Heilner also grew fond of the locals and became a fixture of support, assisting in bringing the island back to life after one of its periodic natural disasters. His cabin cruiser *Nepenthe* made countless trips up and down the eastern seaboard and across the Gulf Stream, pioneering routes now followed by so many others. Above all he fished, experimenting with new tackle and techniques until able to battle the local denizens to a standstill. Always anxious to learn, Heilner also traveled to California and became an early Tuna Club member after winning his coveted gold button in 1921 after three years of trying. While there, his feverish daily competitions with the likes of Zane Grey and Jimmy Jump became the stuff of legend.

73

---

[12] With Frank Stick, a lifelong companion.

[13] Although his enthusiastic practice of harpooning sharks and sunfish "until his arms ached" is difficult to square with this position.

An early view of Bimini and its treacherous harbor entry at top.

With his stock soaring in both writing and angling circles, Heilner was soon appointed Associate Editor of *Field & Stream*, forming a lifelong relationship with the magazine and participating in a variety of its expeditions and research projects. Having undertaken postgraduate studies in ichthyology at the AMNH in his youth, he was no dilettante on the subject of marine science. During his tenure, Heilner conducted much original research and became an accomplished identifier of new species, achievements which further endeared him to *Field & Stream*. In doing so, he also noted a void created by the lack of historical record-keeping, and he recognized that such documentation would not only promulgate the sport but also add significantly to undersea science. Such a woeful need required action, and Heilner proved up to the task.

Heilner's first serious attempt at record-keeping began in the early 1920s. After almost a year of research, he assembled a list of records from various sources and badgered *Field & Stream* into publishing a yearly summary. As an aid to gathering input, he utilized the annual angling contest that the magazine had already been sponsoring for some years. Contest winners would be automatically judged against existing world records and, if possessing a larger catch, would supplant the existing record-holder. If no current record existed for a given species, the largest submission in that category would become the standard-bearer. At first, little consideration was given to angling rules except that any catch submitted for record consideration had to be taken in a sporting manner. As the list of records grew, Heilner enlisted the help of AMNH staffers Francesca LaMonte and John T. Nichols, and an accounting of current record-holders was maintained in a large leather-bound volume in the Museum's Hall of Fishes. It wasn't perfect, but it was a start.

After two decades of almost continuous fishing and writing about fishing, Heilner's reputation hit a zenith with his contribution of two chapters to Derrydale's prestigious publication *American Big Game Fishing* (1935) and the release two years later of his own seminal work *Salt Water Fishing*. The latter became the first best-selling book about angling since Izaak Walton's *The Compleat Angler*.[14] Heilner's vast fishing experience and expertise were well in evidence throughout the book, and his good friend Michael Lerner must have recognized the unique combination of writing, record-keeping, and angling skills that Heilner could bring to a nascent IGFA. With Wylie already designated as the organization's official scribe, that role was filled. However, Heilner's co-stewardship of the *Field & Stream* records would allow a smooth transition in that area, and his credibility as an angler and vast network of contacts were invaluable assets. Besides that, Heilner and Lerner were frequent angling companions and Bimini neighbors. He was the perfect choice to round out the IGFA's inaugural board.[15]

With his organization in place, it was time for war and Lerner turned his attention to WWII.

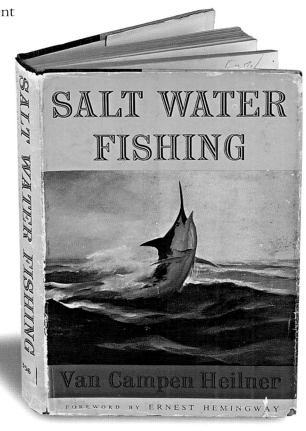

The success of Salt Water Fishing *surprised even its author.*

---

[14] *In its two early printings,* Salt Water Fishing *included forwards from such luminaries as Zane Grey and Ernest Hemingway.*

[15] *Heilner later became somewhat disillusioned after WWII as angling pressure exploded and the virgin seas became fewer. Nevertheless, he remained a dedicated inshore enthusiast (his first love) and is best known today for his graceful waxings on surf fishing that appeared in various publications.*

Mike Lerner demonstrates his emergency fishing kit to various branches of the American armed service during World War II.

Chapter Four

ANGLERS AT WAR

MICHAEL LERNER COULD SCARCELY HAVE PICKED a more difficult year to found the IGFA. The world was coming to blows in 1939, with the tides of war rising on every sea. In March, Germany invaded the Czech Republic, overrunning its defenders in less than a day and putting the rest of Europe on notice of what was to come. By the fall, Italy and Germany were allies, Poland had been torn apart by the Nazi juggernaut, and all of Europe was at war. Even as the IGFA was meeting for the first time on June 7th, Estonia and Latvia were being cowed into signing non-aggression pacts with the German Reich. It was a sobering time, but the IGFA's founding and its commitment to international sportsmanship were slivers of hope in a world gone mad.

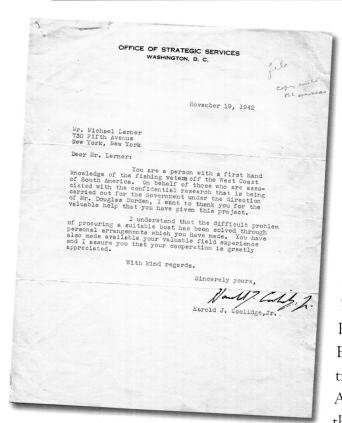

IGFA files are silent as to exactly what this intriguing 1942 letter is about, but it likely refers to the research on survival at sea that Lerner was beginning to undertake. The OSS was America's primary intelligence-gathering unit during WWII and was later succeeded by the CIA.

On December 7, 1941, the Japanese attack at Pearl Harbor finally put America into the war. Early battlefield losses were heavy as the country scrambled to mobilize, especially in the US Navy and Army Air Force. As Allied planes were lost over the Pacific, stories began to emerge of airmen adrift at sea for weeks under the most harrowing of circumstances. In November 1942, World War I Ace Eddie Rickenbacker, his aide Colonel H.C. Adamson and others were lost at sea for 21 days following a navigational error in the South Pacific. With little to eat or drink, he and his crew drifted for nearly 500 miles before being rescued on the island of Tuvalu. Similarly, Brigadier General Nathan Twining's[1] forced landing of his Flying Fortress at sea near the Solomon Islands averted tragedy only by the narrowest of margins. In the South Atlantic, Navy seaman Basil Izzi and two companions found themselves adrift for 83 days after their ship was torpedoed and sunk. Izzi was reduced to wriggling his toes in the water to attract sharks, a risky but ultimately successful proposition. In these cases and many others, the survival gear the men found themselves with proved to be virtually useless.

As such accounts began to reach the Life Saving Board of the Navy and Coast Guard, pressure grew rapidly to improve the survival chances of

---

[1] *In 1957, Twining would be appointed Chairman of the Joint Chiefs of Staff by President Dwight Eisenhower.*

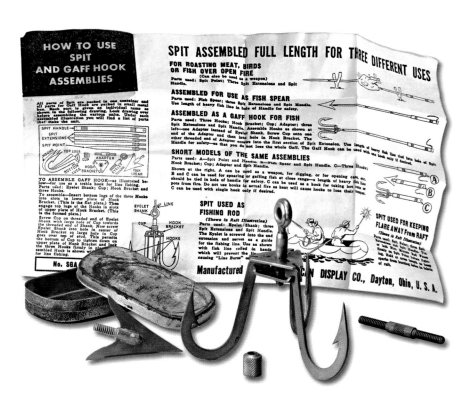

This early-war survival kit from the Army Air Force offered little of value to pilots downed at sea.

downed pilots and torpedoed sailors. The Board approached ichthyologist-turned-Pennsylvania Governor Gifford Pinchot for advice, and Pinchot in turn consulted with Dr. Alexander Wetmore of the Smithsonian Institution. When the two men looked at the current state of the military's life-saving equipment, they quickly realized that much of it dated to the era of sail. Wetmore knew of Mike Lerner and was aware that Lerner was looking for ways in which the IGFA could aid in the Allied war effort. His subsequent introduction of Lerner to Pinchot would prove to be pivotal.

Upon learning of the crisis, Lerner immediately jumped at the invitation to assist in the design of a new survival kit for servicemen adrift at sea. Pinchot had already done considerable research on the edibility of saltwater fish, and he had determined that all but four relatively rare species could be safely eaten either cooked or raw. He had also discovered how a lymphatic fluid could be extracted from the flesh of raw fish and substituted for water. Indeed, subsequent tests showed that sailors could easily survive for 10 days or more while drinking nothing else. With this information in hand, a technical committee was formed in late 1942, with Lerner at its head, to address the need for an improved emergency survival kit. Its members were among the most accomplished anglers of the day — Lerner, Kip Farrington, Philip Wylie, Captain Eddie Wall, Julian Crandall, and Captain Bill Hatch — and it immediately went to work.

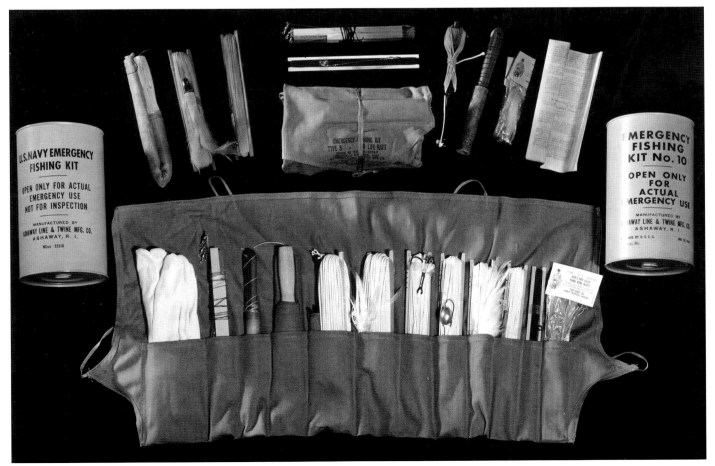

An exploded view of the Emergency Fishing Kit used by Allied maritime services in all theatres of the war.

Recognizing the vital and immediate importance of its charge, the group interviewed hundreds of airmen and sailors with the first-hand experience of being abandoned at sea. Lerner himself spent months testing various elements off the coast of Florida, and all committee members participated in extensive sea trials. In February of 1943, the new kit was formally adopted by the US Navy and shortly thereafter by the other maritime services. Instead of the heavy tarred lines used previously, Lerner introduced the concept of an emergency vest that included hooks of various sizes, assorted baits, a knife, sharpening stone, net, harpoon, and (most importantly) instructions for use. Packed in a sealed coffee can and weighing about three pounds, each element in the kit was carefully described and its use outlined in a variety of different settings. The pursuit of fish over 50 lb was discouraged since a loss of gear could be catastrophic. Nevertheless, servicemen were instructed as to the capture of birds, bait, turtles, crawfish, and anything else that might keep them alive.

Ashaway was founded in 1824 by Lester Crandall, a frustrated fishing smack captain who could never find enough suitable line and twine for his nets. An innovator from the beginning, Crandall was soon producing a superior cotton twine used by commercial fishermen up and down the Northeast coast. With the advent of surfcasting around 1840, the prevailing cotton line proved inadequate so Crandall came up with the idea of a twisted linen line that would actually gain strength when immersed in salt water. Ultimately, his Original Cuttyhunk Linen Line became the premier brand name among recreational fishing lines and was sought after by anglers for nearly 100 years. Each linen thread was hand-twisted into line inside a famously unheated 725' line "walk" attached to the main warehouse along the Ashaway River. Crandall and his family successors devised all the machines and techniques used in manufacturing and would later pioneer both the waterproofing of silk lines and the development of synthetic nylon line. Indeed, Ashaway was among DuPont's first and largest buyers of nylon and did much to identify its unique characteristics. Under the able wartime leadership of Julian Crandall (great grandson of Lester), Ashaway became a key supplier of nylon war material, including hammock cords, parachute shrouds, surgical sutures, tow ropes, and many other items. After the war, Ashaway resumed fishing line production and Crandall vigorously lobbied the IGFA to accept synthetic line for purposes of world record consideration. However, despite their considerable experience, Ashaway was ultimately forced out of the fishing line business by lower cost manufacturers and today contents itself with producing line for tennis and racquetball racquets.

A serviceman demonstrates proper technique in using the Emergency Fishing Kit developed by Lerner and his committee.

A selection of items found in the smaller survival kit issued to Allied airmen.

Once approved, the kits were constructed by Julian Crandall and his Ashaway Line & Twine Company in Ashaway, Rhode Island (see sidebar on page 80).[2] In short order, they were packed aboard lifeboats and ship's rafts and began saving lives almost immediately. Literally hundreds of grateful letters were received from servicemen in all theatres, prompting several other Allied nations to adopt the kits and also hastening the development of a smaller kit especially for downed airmen that could be packed aboard an emergency life raft.

The near overnight success of the military survival kits brought enormous acclaim to the IGFA, and this quickly spawned another project. In many remote outposts, wounded servicemen at field hospitals had little to do during their recovery, and patient morale was correspondingly poor. After some consideration, it was decided that taking advantage of local angling opportunities might represent both a welcome distraction and a means of supplementing military rations. In early 1943, Lerner first proposed the idea of a recreational fishing kit to authorities in Washington DC, but he soon grew frustrated after months of governmental foot-dragging. Determined to see his idea through, he personally financed the development and initial production of what would quickly become a hugely successful morale-builder. The first recreational kits consisted of 100 feet of 30-lb test fishing line, assorted lures, hooks, and sinkers, plus a spearhead, dip net, and

---

[2]While Ashaway was the primary supplier, some kits were made by Horrocks-Ibbotson of Utica, New York.

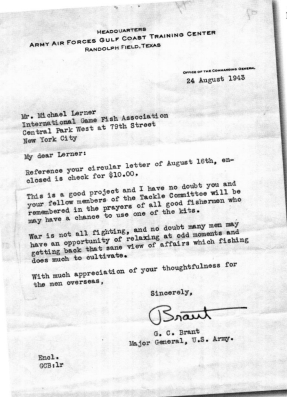

As evidenced by this letter from Major General Brant, even the Army brass contributed to the IGFA's appeal for funds.

instructions printed on waterproof paper. The contents were then wrapped in a twill sleeve and made ready for shipment. Weighing in at a tidy 41 ounces, their worth to wounded servicemen quickly proved more than gold.

The IGFA teamed up with the Red Cross to facilitate distribution, and the first 3,000 kits prompted a flood of letters pleading for more. Among many others were the following (printed as received):

Dear Sir:

As I was reading a newspaper today I came across this clipping about a fishing kit. Where I am on an island it sure is good fishing and I love to fish. I fish with mason line and for a hook I use a piece of welding wire, but haven't got a file to make a sharp point. I would appreciate a kit if you have any left. I am willing to pay for it at any cost. So if you haven't any will you drop me a line and tell me where I can get some. I haven't been back in the States in 19 months and don't think I can come till the war is over in Europe.

s/ Robert J. Palmer, S 2/c (sgd)

Dear Sir:

I read an article in my home town paper where you are going to send a fishing tackle kit for men overseas. I am a native of Wisconsin, therefore a fisherman. Of late I have been spending my off time on the ocean beaches. Tho the Aussies are free to loan me their "gear" I'm mighty clumsy in using it as it is quite different from ours. Now I have the angler's fever so am trying to obtain some good old U.S.A. tackle.

If it is at all possible, I'd greatly appreciate you sending me one of your kits. I'm more than willing to pay for a set and also an extra set so that some other angler might benefit by your thoughtfulness.

Hoping to hear from you soon.

s/ Sgt Roy Miller

Dear Mr. Lerner:

(excerpted) While stationed in the Gulf of Aden in 1941 I'd have given my eye teeth for one of your fishing kits as the sea teemed with fish of all kinds. I managed to buy a length of very inferior white line for an exhorbitant (sic) price from an Arab and made fish hooks from bully beef tin keys. With a few pieces of paraffin, tin and some solder I fashioned a queer looking spinner but queer as it was it was no mean lure, and was snapped off, second throw in, by some large fish. Tuna are not known to South African fishermen except from books and museums, but I reckon, these fish up to 150 lbs., were small tuna — yellowfin. Ever(y) bait thrown in was snapped up and my weak line broke each time like cotton- how I longed for a set of decent tackle!

s/ Lt. A.J.F. Low

In virtually all theatres of operation, the results were glowing and multi-faceted. Diet, morale, and recreational diversity improved dramatically among the recipients, and a national fund-raising campaign was enacted by the IGFA Tackle Committee to meet the demand. Once again, Ashaway Line & Twine stepped up to manufacture the kits (at a cost of $2 apiece), and Lerner himself paid for the entire initial production run. Ernest Hemingway was cajoled into writing a letter in support of donations, and Lerner wrote a series of personal appeals to his sporting friends around the world. Additional monies were raised by a nonprofit corporation based in Miami called the Armed Forces Fishing Committee, for which Lerner also served as a director. The recreational angling kits were ultimately adopted by the Special Services Division of the War Department and produced in enormous numbers.[3] By war's end, it was estimated that more than one million returning servicemen had been introduced to angling through the efforts of Lerner and the IGFA.

---

[3] *By the end of the war, Ashaway had manufactured more than 200,000 such kits.*

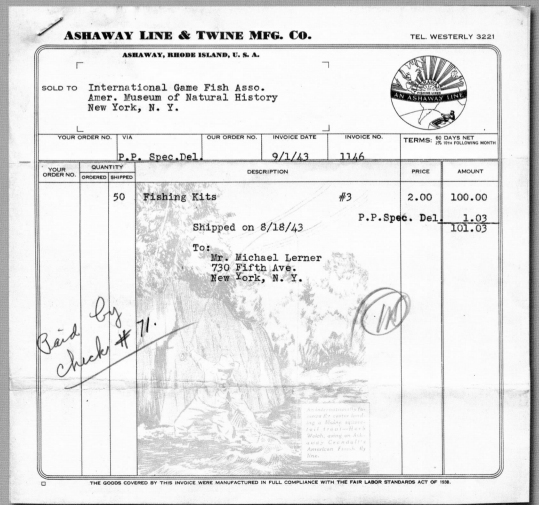

This invoice, and many like it, were received and was paid by Lerner himself to kick off production of the recreational fishing kits.

Captain Eddie Wall (standing at left) and servicemen stationed on Ascension Island with a nice day's catch.

As word trickled in from many parts of the world, Lerner kept an interested ear pealed for new fishing hotspots. Soldiers caught salmon and trout in Scotland, kingfish in Curacao, and a dazzling array of tropical species in the Pacific. Upon hearing a report that Allied servicemen based on remote Ascension Island (a key airbase supplying Allied troops in North Africa) were living on canned goods and K-rations, he dispatched his personal captain Eddie Wall to explore the surrounding waters. Wall found virgin fishing grounds for tuna, wahoo, and almost every pelagic species imaginable, and a fishing program was enacted that combined both recreational and subsistence elements. Soon afterwards, Lerner was pleased to hear that the diet of local servicemen had improved considerably.

Fishing activity by servicemen on remote atolls also served to build bonds with the natives. In one locale, heretofore passive islanders grew restless while watching a soldier fish without success in a Pacific lagoon. Finally, they approached him and through sign language made him aware that he was fishing in the wrong place and using the wrong bait. After adjusting his technique as suggested, his success rate soared. Many similar interactions and not a few friendships between natives and servicemen grew from like circumstances.

Despite his satisfaction at the success of the angling kits, Lerner ached to do more for the war effort and he finally had another chance. The American press had always been generous to Lerner and his diminutive wife Helen, and their joint fishing and hunting exploits had been widely celebrated in the media. As a result, when they were asked to join one of the famous USO Camp Shows as volunteer guest personalities, they both eagerly accepted. Such shows were held throughout the war to maintain morale, and many leading entertainers of the day participated (most notably Bob Hope). These shows were not without hazard as some 17 performers were killed in the line of duty, including Big Band leader Glenn Miller who was killed in a 1944 plane crash on his way to Paris. Nevertheless, by war's end nearly 300,000 Camp Show performances had been held in more than 42 countries, entertaining millions of troops in a manner completely unknown to earlier conflicts. Among the most enthusiastic personalities were Helen and Michael Lerner who told stories of battles with giant fish to servicemen fresh from the Italian front. Punctuated with photos and tackle, their tales were spellbinding to the exhausted soldiers.[4]

---

[4]*After the war, the USO asked the Lerners to go back to Italy and North Africa to gauge the angling interest of servicemen posted overseas. Their stories and tackle demonstrations drew enormous crowds.*

The Lerners show off their tackle (and Helen her dazzling smile) during their USO tour of Italy in 1945.

Despite often being shy and inarticulate in public, Lerner came alive in front of these servicemen. He had a masterful memory, and his time as a young traveling salesman had given him great familiarity with the particulars of many small towns. During the course of the evening, Lerner would ask the lonely young men about their families and neighborhoods. When he came across someone from a small town that he knew, Lerner would often be able to recall such local details as street names and other landmarks. By that time, Lerner Stores were dotted throughout America and Mike Lerner was one of the most famous sportsmen in the world. He was widely recognized as a celebrity, yet he could relate to those sailors and soldiers in a manner that few other entertainers could. With Mike's personal touch and Helen's dazzling smile, the troops were captivated.[5]

[5] *Later, Kip Farrington and his wife Chisie also toured military bases in the Pacific to rave reviews.*

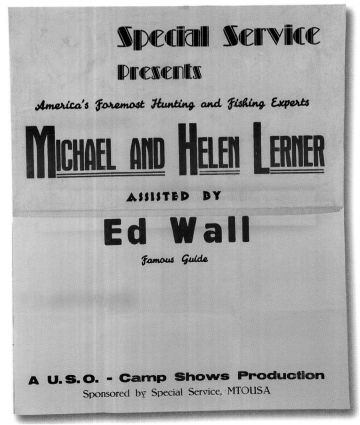

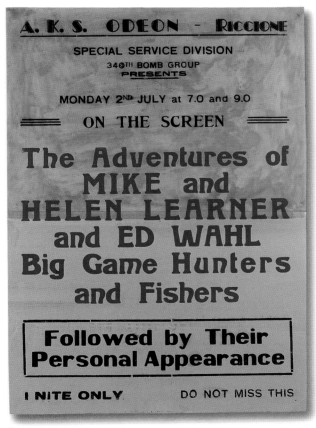

Posters like these promoted the Lerners' USO appearances throughout their tour.

INTERNATIONAL GAME FISH ASSOCIATION
THE AMERICAN MUSEUM OF NATURAL HISTORY
CENTRAL PARK WEST AT 79TH STREET

NEW YORK, N. Y.

OFFICERS AND EXECUTIVE COMMITTEE

PRESIDENT: WILLIAM K. GREGORY PH. D., SC. D., CURATOR OF ICHTHYOLOGY	VICE-PRESIDENT: VAN CAMPEN HEILNER FIELD REPRESENTATIVE, DEPT. OF ICHTHYOLOGY	FIELD REPRESENTATIVE: PHILIP WYLIE SECRETARY: FRANCESCA LAMONTE
VICE-PRESIDENT: MICHAEL LERNER FIELD ASSOCIATE, DEPT. OF ICHTHYOLOGY	VICE-PRESIDENT: ERNEST HEMINGWAY	ASSOCIATE CURATOR, DEPT. OF ICHTHYOLOGY

TACKLE COMMITTEE:

TO PROVIDE RECREATIONAL FISHING KITS FOR MEN IN SERVICE OVERSEAS
MICHAEL LERNER, CHAIRMAN   PHILIP WYLIE, VICE CHAIRMAN

August 12, 1943

Mr. Gene Tunney
United States Marines
Washington, D.C.

Dear Gene:

As a fellow sportsman I am sending you under separate cover, with my compliments, one of the fishing kits which we hope to place in the hands of every overseas serviceman who wants to go fishing during his time off between bullets, bombs and barrages.

The American public has provided all manner of entertainment for our Armed Forces in this country but what about the boys overseas who are deprived of everyday enjoyments.

Millions of our boys are stationed where recreation is limited. And yet, in most places one of the finest sports---good fishing---is available. We know many of these boys often try to improvise fishing hooks from discarded wire, scraps of metal and even safety pins.

We want to provide tackle for them and have designed a practical fishing kit suitable for both salt and fresh water fishing. Wont you show the kit to your friends and enlist their enthusiastic support. Every additional kit means more relaxation for our fighting men. Each kit costs only $2.00 and will be used by many boys. Every dollar contributed will be spent for fishing kits only. Campaign expenses are donated by this organization. The American Red Cross has assumed complete distribution of the kits.

The International Game Fish Association is sponsoring a drive to raise funds for the manufacture of these kits on a non-profit basis and I have started the ball rolling by contributing the first thousand kits.

Here's a chance for sportsmen of America to do an outstanding job for those boys who are sacrificing so much for our country. Anything you send will be appreciated. Make checks payable to Michael Lerner, Chairman, at the above address.

Sincerely

Michael Lerner

P.S. Contributions may be deducted from your income tax.

Ex-heavyweight boxing champion Gene Tunney was an avid angler and friend to Lerner and the IGFA. Here, Lerner calls on Tunney to assist in the fund-raising effort for the IGFA's recreational fishing kits. After the war, Tunney served on the IGFA's Executive Committee.

Despite their strenuous war-related efforts, Lerner and the IGFA also remained hard at work on their organizational agenda. The IGFA's original structure provided for affiliations with other institutions and clubs, and much effort was given to establishing these relationships. By 1943, the count had increased to six scientific institutions, 27 member clubs, and 25 International Representatives. The early Representatives were an august group, including Charles M. Cooke III (of the Cooke Trust Company) in Hawaii, W.E.S. Tuker (manager of the Anglo-Chilean Nitrate Company) in Chile, Dr. Harold Pettit (a prominent New Zealand physician), and Sir Arnold Hodson, Governor of Africa's Gold Coast. This group proved critical in helping to create the IGFA's first-ever yearbook in 1943, as much of this early publication was given over to Representative descriptions of fishing conditions in various parts of the world. From that first overview, it was clear that the war was taking its toll on recreational angling.

88

Mike Lerner and two military escorts tour the Italian theatre in 1945.

Helen Lerner and company in Italy (1945).

In 1943, WWII was raging in both the European and Pacific theatres, and virtually all well-known fishing locales had been affected. In Nigeria, IGFA Representative J.N. Zarpas reported that the country's one fishing cruiser was presently "trolling these waters for other than tarpon." In South Africa, fishing opportunities were restricted as war authorities banned angling from wharves and jetties. Fishing was at a complete standstill in Australia as their war effort consumed all available resources, and New Zealand bemoaned the lack of American anglers seen during more normal times. The report submitted by the Representative from the British West Indies was so heavily censored by local authorities that little of interest remained. Perhaps worst affected was the Philippines, as almost the entire lot of IGFA correspondents there had been imprisoned or killed by the Japanese. In its list of member clubs, the IGFA showed the Philippine Game Fishing Association as "suspended during occupation".

One letter to Lerner from R.L. Marston in Kent, England dated March 1, 1944 was particularly vivid:

> *Although the renewed air attacks on London are not comparable with the early blitz or with our bombing of Germany, they are sufficiently nerve wracking to be tiresome to say the least. I doubt if one would ever get used to the tension of listening when planes are overhead amidst the noise of the barrage. One hears all kinds of strange noises: bits of anti-aircraft shells whining down or maybe empty flare cases, and occasionally the whine and crump of a bomb, even once or twice the roar as a plane crashes. One good feature of the present raids is that, however sharp they may be, they are usually pretty short and do not last more than an hour or so. The shorter the better as far as I personally am concerned, as waiting for something that may come down does not appeal to me a bit.*

Despite a serious war-related paper shortage and the required vetting by the wartime Office of Censorship, the release of its 112-page yearbook in 1943 was a critical milestone for the IGFA. While acknowledging the ongoing war effort, the book was upbeat and optimistic in its assessment of the "world-wide fraternity of game fishermen." The IGFA's early years had been most formative, and the yearbook included (among other things) the first set of standardized rules ever promulgated for big-game fishing, an angler's reading list, and even a brief ichthyological history of big-game fish written by Gregory. Some 5,000 copies of this inaugural book were printed, and they were distributed free of charge upon request. Despite the wartime circumstances, inquiries poured in from around the world and supplies were quickly exhausted.

The Lerners' trophy room in their New York City apartment was the scene of many social events for returning servicemen during WWII.

Always a man of rigorous principles, Lerner refused to fish aboard power boats after Pearl Harbor so as not to take gasoline away from the war effort.[6] Nevertheless, he fished locally from piers and docks near his home in Miami and commuted to New York for IGFA and war-related business. Occasionally, Lerner threw parties for servicemen in his incredible trophy room in New York City, a legendary display that occupied the entire 23rd floor of a prominent building on Fifth Avenue. Soldiers were known to gawk for hours at the dozens of heads, skins, and trophies. Throughout the war, Lerner also carried on an extensive correspondence with servicemen he had met over the course of his travels, and he especially enjoyed hearing about one GI catching an 80 lb kingfish using tackle from one of Lerner's kits, a world record if taken on conventional tackle. In that soldier, Lerner knew he had a fisherman for life.

---

[6]*Even though OPA restrictions were relaxed near the end of the war to allow for power boat fishing.*

As the war began to wind down in 1945, shortages of both fuel and tackle began to lessen and many new fishing clubs were formed or reconstituted. Nevertheless, while Lerner was being showered with kudos for his wartime efforts, the IGFA began to realize that it had a problem. Having taken over the record-keeping duties previously held by *Field & Stream* magazine and the American Museum of Natural History, it soon became apparent that a number of its inherited records were incomplete, largely undocumented, or inconsistent with the IGFA's original rules.[7] Just as the war was ending, a multi-year review of existing records was undertaken and the IGFA went to enormous lengths to document early record claims. Claimants and witnesses were contacted, old files were exhaustively reviewed, and finally in 1949 a number of records were retired as simply unproven. Nevertheless, the organization remained open to their reinstatement and invited all interested parties to come forward if they could verify the claim. Some did, and a handful of records were reinstated. The rest simply went away.

Few organizations born in the shadow of war can overcome such a handicap and survive. That the International Game Fish Association not only survived its untimely birth but contributed so much to the Allied war effort is an achievement that cannot be overstated. In the process, thousands of lives were saved and millions of new anglers created, fueling a post-war boom in recreational fishing that continues to this day. With the conversion back to a peace-time economy, new advances in tackle also helped to encourage angling. Fiberglass soon replaced bamboo in rod making, nylon line rapidly overtook linen, and wartime advances in metallurgy helped spur the production of saltwater fishing reels. Nevertheless, even the rosiest forecaster could not have predicted the incredible angling successes that were just around the corner.

---

[7] *For example, many early record fish were shot at the point of capture, a common old-time practice used to subdue large fish.*

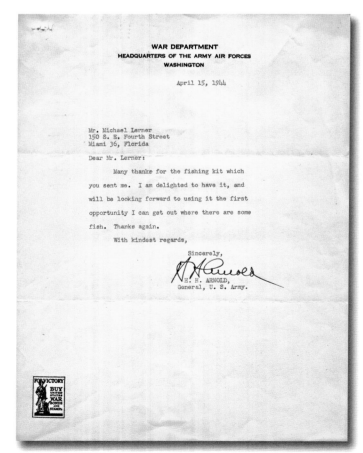

Lerner's public relations savvy also showed itself in his mailing of recreational kits to a number of general officers, including legendary Army General H.H. "Hap" Arnold.

THE COMMANDING GENERAL
AIR DEFENSE COMMAND
MITCHEL FIELD, NEW YORK

Dear Mr. Lerner:

It has been a great pleasure for me to present you with the President's Certificate of Merit on this, the 4th day of February, nineteen hundred and forty-eight, at Mitchel Air Force Base.

In behalf of all the airmen under my command during World War II, I too wish to thank you for your outstanding services in designing and producing life saving and fishing kits which resulted in the saving of many lives during combat.

Sincerely,

Geo. E. Stratemeyer

GEORGE E. STRATEMEYER
Lieutenant General, U. S. Air Force
Commanding

One of many commendation letters received by Lerner for his outstanding contributions to the Allied war effort.

Zane Grey admires his 758 lb Atlantic bluefin tuna taken off Wedgeport, Nova Scotia in 1924.

Chapter Five

BIG GAME IN DISTANT SEAS

As the world put itself back together after WWII, the IGFA began a similar period of change and growth. In many regions, a resumption of recreational angling was hampered by an acute shortage of tackle, but that shortage began to ease as factories converted back to peace-time production. In its first post-war yearbook released in 1948, the IGFA could boast of having 80 member clubs (triple the wartime number) and representation in more than 44 different nations and territories. More importantly, due in part to far-flung travel by IGFA officials, the organization had solidified its position as the world's foremost big-game fishing authority. By then, its legitimacy as the clearinghouse for world record claims was unchallenged, and correspondence began to pour in as angling efforts increased.

The 1948 yearbook also documented a number of internal changes within the IGFA. During the war, Michael Lerner had assumed the IGFA Presidency from William Gregory (who remained active as President Emeritus), and noted screenwriter and author Phillip Wylie had been appointed First Vice President. In addition, a most impressive angling trio of B.D. Crowninshield, Van Campen Heilner, and Ernest Hemingway had been appointed Vice Presidents. With the indispensable Francesca LaMonte continuing as Secretary, the IGFA's leadership and organization would change little in the following 12 years as big-game angling entered a golden age of unprecedented growth and colossal accomplishments. From 1948 until Michael Lerner stepped down as IGFA President, the story was all about the fishing.

During that early post-war period, the big-game angling fraternity was at most a thousand strong. At the very top, those with the will and means to go anywhere in the world in pursuit of ever-larger fish numbered perhaps a few dozen. The great ones were household names in angling circles: William Carpenter, Julian Crandall, Ben Crowninshield, Kip Farrington, Alfred C. Glassell Jr., Tony Hulman, Michael Lerner, Hal Lyman, Lou Marron, Julio Sanchez, Tommy Shevlin, and a dozen others. Ultimately, those were the men that defined the sport. They pioneered the destinations, inspired the development of new tackle and techniques, and promoted the rules and ethics of angling as defined by the IGFA. To understand the incredible fishing of the day is to understand their enthusiasm and commitment to the sport.

World-class angler Julio Sanchez leans into a big fish. Sanchez also helped design the fighting chair footrest and bucket harness, both enormously helpful to heavy-tackle anglers.

Kip Farrington, captain of the American Tuna Team, congratulates British angler Louis Mowbray during the first International Tuna Cup Match held in Wedgeport (1937).

What is often described as a post-war angling boom was actually well underway by the early 1930s. The Miami charter boat fleet was growing and healthy, and budding recreational fisheries in the Bahamas, Mexico, and elsewhere were starting to emerge. As new anglers gained experience in Florida waters, they began to look outward for greater challenges, and nowhere were these challenges more bountiful than Wedgeport (Nova Scotia), Bimini (Bahamas), and Cabo Blanco (Peru). Each location had a stand-out species: Wedgeport with its fat Atlantic bluefin tuna, Bimini with its powerful blue marlin, and Cabo Blanco with its massive black marlin. In short order, these three very different regions of the world would become legendary in angling circles and would collectively come to symbolize the golden era of big-game fishing.

WEDGEPORT, NOVA SCOTIA (CANADA)

Long known as a home to giant Atlantic bluefin tuna, Wedgeport saw few recreational anglers of note until Zane Grey made a pilgrimage there in 1924. However, his rod-and-reel capture of a 758 lb specimen in Jordan Bay was seen as a fluke and largely ignored. Grey's constant self-promotion had already begun to irritate many of his contemporaries, and few could afford his lavish investment in suitable tackle. Indeed, little tackle was available at any price that could stand up to such punishment, and virtually none of it was in Nova Scotia. Thus, when he left, commercial fishermen went back to harpooning these enormous "horse mackerel" in the traditional way and little more was thought of it.

Nevertheless, it was a different story 11 years later when Michael Lerner appeared on the scene. His capture of giant bluefin tuna off the famous Soldier's Rip some 45 minutes from Wedgeport galvanized the angling world and created a veritable stampede. Lerner's preference was to fish from a small skiff towed behind a larger motorboat. When a giant tuna would strike, the skiff was released and the fish would tow the small

A day's catch off Miami's legendary Pier 5 (1940).

boat around in a manner that soon became known as a Wedgeport "sleigh ride."[1] It was tremendously exciting, but not for the faint of heart. Nevertheless, the idea thrilled a small but growing number of largely American anglers who had cut their teeth on Florida marlin and sailfish. New advances in tackle promised to prolong such battles with these leviathans, and transportation alternatives to the remote northeast coast of Canada were improving. Thus, Wedgeport became the first great angling destination for those in pursuit of the world's largest fish.

After Mike Lerner's success put Wedgeport on the map, it fell to Kip Farrington to assure Wedgeport's place in angling history. Born in 1904 into a successful New Jersey clan, Farrington spent seven years in the family stock brokerage firm before leaving to pursue a vagabond's life of writing, railroading and big-game angling. For the next 10 years, he became a fixture among the small cadre of dedicated big-game anglers, helping to pioneer Bimini in the early 1930s and ultimately writing more than two dozen books over a long and productive career. Fiercely independent, Farrington never settled for a desk job but chose to publish regularly in many leading magazines and later served as Salt Water Editor for *Field & Stream* magazine from 1937-1972. He met and married his wife Sarah Chisholm (known to all as "Chisie") in 1934 and she would ultimately become one of the most accomplished female anglers of her day. Both would play a major role in elevating Wedgeport to world renown.

Chisie Farrington with a 673 lb tuna taken in Wedgeport (1946). The fish set a 24-thread (linen) world record for women.

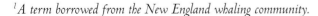

[1] *A term borrowed from the New England whaling community.*

Neither the weather nor the boats at Wedgeport were known for their comfort.

The victorious Cuban team (1947). From left are Frederico Mejer, Captain Julio Sanchez, Mario Menocal, and Thorvald Sanchez.

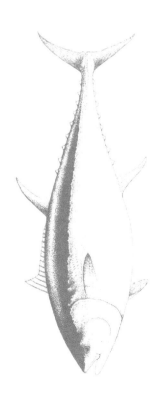

While participating in a number of international fishing competitions in the mid-1930s, Farrington conceived the idea of a Canadian tournament focused on the Atlantic bluefin tuna. Enlisting the help of Mike Lerner, he worked tirelessly for two years to bring the idea to life. In 1937, the first International Tuna Cup Match was held in Wedgeport and went on to become the most successful big-game angling tournament of its era. Later known as the Sharp Cup,[2] the annual event ran for more than 40 years and eventually included almost every big-game angler of world stature. Farrington's genius was in formatting the event after the venerable Davis Cup matches in tennis. From the beginning, the Sharp Cup was an international team competition with the original contest held between the British Empire and the United States of America. On the heels of a hurricane that first year, the British Empire team found itself one angler short on opening day and was forced to borrow New York angler Lee Wulff.[3] Ultimately, Wulff's two fish won the event for the British, and the unique competitive spirit of the Sharp Cup was underway.

The following year, the event was moved to Liverpool, Nova Scotia but returned in 1939 to Wedgeport where it would stay for good.

---

[2] *For the winner's trophy donated by Alton B. Sharp of the Eastern Steamship Line.*

[3] *Among many other angling accomplishments, Wulff captured the first large tuna off Newfoundland in 1938, invented the fly-fishing vest (1931), created countless fly patterns that remain in use today, and set several long-lived IGFA world records. Also a superb fly fisher, his widow Joan became an IGFA Trustee in 2001.*

World War II interrupted the competition until 1947, but it reemerged with a vengeance and ultimately included teams from 19 different countries. Chisie Farrington served in the critical role of Match Scorekeeper for the event's first 11 years, and Kip himself was part of the victorious American teams in 1948 and 1949. Indeed, 1949 proved to be the greatest year ever for tuna fishing off Nova Scotia as hundreds of giant tuna were landed on rod and reel, a staggering 72 of which were taken by just five teams during the three days of Sharp Cup competition. However, the following year's tournament saw only eight tuna taken, and fishing dwindled steadily thereafter. In 1959, the event was finally cancelled, and although later re-started it never again achieved the magic of earlier years. Nevertheless, the Sharp Cup remains one of the most pivotal big-game angling tournaments ever held and did more for Nova Scotia tourism than any other single event before or since. It was also among the first major tournaments to substantially adopt IGFA rules as tournament angling standards, and it will forever be remembered as a pacesetter for that reason among many others.

Canadian teammates congratulate Lee Wulff on landing the winning tuna during the first Sharp Cup (1937).

Sharp Cup participants at Wedgeport (1947).

BIMINI, BAHAMAS

Situated some 50 miles due east of Miami, the tropical paradise of Bimini lies on the edge of the American continental shelf and adjacent to the great Gulf Stream current. Here the Gulf Stream moves south-to-north at about five knots, ultimately carrying a stream of warm water along with a collection of pelagic game fish more than 2,500 miles. So extensive is the Gulf Stream flow that anglers even in the adjacent northern latitudes are able to pursue warmwater game fish in its midst throughout the year. What is noteworthy is that this pelagic highway is barely a stone's throw from Bimini, itself already home to more than 600 species of marine fish. As one of the world's earliest big-game fishing destinations, its history and that of the IGFA are closely intertwined.

Originally sought by Ponce de Leon as the legendary source of the Fountain of Youth, Bimini never did play host to this famous explorer but his accidental discovery of Florida in 1513 would change the world. First claimed by Spain and later seized by the British, Bimini became a pivotal reprovisioning port for all manner of explorers, traders, and pirates. In the early 1920s, it was transformed into a rollicking outpost for those wishing to avoid stateside Prohibition. Business was good, with extra excitement provided by the occasional gun battle between "revenuers" and "scofflaws." Things settled down for a time with the repeal of Prohibition, but the onslaught of big-game anglers in search of a new kind of thrill was just over the horizon.

The windswept island of Bimini as viewed from the roof of the Compleat Angler hostelry (ca. 1935).

Captain Tommy Gifford and his boat Lady Grace *brought many big fish to the Bimini dock.*

The first blue marlin to be taken off Bimini is variously attributed to different anglers in the early 1930s, but it seems clear than Van Campen Heilner caught (or at least tangled with) the first billfish some years before. Not wanting to disturb his private bonefish sanctuary, Heilner remained mum about the island's offshore potential throughout the 1920s until finally letting the angling world in on the secret. Once the news was out, Kip Farrington, Ernest Hemingway and Mike Lerner were among the first to ply Bimini's virgin offshore waters. When fishing legend Tommy Gifford did some exploratory fishing in 1933 with Cat Cay owner Lou Wasey, his capture of a 501 lb blue marlin ensured that the rush was on. Soon, giant tuna and other game fish were discovered nearby, and the latter half of the 1930s saw an unprecedented boom in offshore fishing excitement. Dozens of adventurous anglers were drawn to the new sport, and Bimini quickly became the nucleus for big-game angling worldwide. Unlike Wedgeport, the island was pleasantly warm, fairly close to civilization, and needed only some decent accommodations to make it the perfect hotspot. That final need was met when the Dower House Hotel opened in 1935, hosting none other than Michael Lerner as its inaugural guest. The Dower House burned to ashes later that year but reopened in 1935 as The Compleat Angler, a name that would become synonymous with island hospitality for decades.

Tommy Gifford

The first blue marlin of note ever taken off Bimini, this 502 lb fish was hooked by Ann Moore and fought by Cat Cay host Lou Wasey. Its capture in March of 1933 created a stampede of big-game anglers to the Bahamas. Wasey is pictured at right with legendary Captain Tommy Gifford at left.

Just as things were really starting to roll, WWII intervened and brought angling on the island to a virtual standstill. Nevertheless, Bimini's proximity to Florida's east coast allowed big-game fishing to resume quickly after the war. Many noted anglers were anxious to reacquaint themselves with the nearly 700 islands in the Bahamas, and Bimini's western-most location and proximity to the Gulf Stream made it an obvious first stop. In 1946, George Lyon's *Alberta* captured 14 tuna to 700 lb during the peak May/June season, and were it not for problems of poor weather and repeated tackle failure, the following year would have been even better. Tarpon, permit, bonefish, and snook had also been discovered inshore, and a number of impressive catches of each were widely heralded. Sailfish were so common as to be rarely fished; most were taken by accident on the heavy tackle set out for bigger game.

Bimini had become the new angler's mecca, and it appeared that no place else could match it.

In addition to a staggering variety of fish, Bimini's waters were also yielding great quality. Just as big-game angling was finding itself in the Bahamas, fishing for tuna and swordfish off Catalina took a decided turn for the worse and most of the records set in California were soundly beaten off Bimini.[4] This inflamed the Florida media, and much was made of each new record catch. *Miami Herald* columnist Erl Roman quickly became a fixture on the local angling scene, trumpeting each new record and often gaining front-page space if tournaments or celebrities were involved (preferably both). New techniques and tackle also evolved as anglers sought to improve their chances against these outsized fish. Such advances as the Bimini twist (used to create a double line), lightweight outriggers and tuna towers made of aluminum, nylon rod harnesses and belts, and the pedestal-style fighting chair all were conceived or improved during this period.

The ravenous sharks off Bimini were always a problem. Captain Bill Fagen inspects a half-eaten catch.

[4]*Striped marlin were taken in good numbers off Catalina during this period, but not of record size.*

Another Bimini record-setter, this 636 lb blue marlin was taken by premier angler Tommy Shevlin in 1935. Surrounding the fish are (from left) artist Lynn Bogue Hunt, Shevlin, Captain Bill Fagen, and Ernest Hemingway.

FOUR GIANT MARLIN DISPLAYED AT ONE TIME AT BIMINI

Four giant marlin with a combined weight of 1,552 pounds and the largest tipping the beam at 478 pounds, were displayed at one time recently in Bimini. All four were taken on rod and reel, and it is the first time in the history of big game fishing that four blue marlin of this large size ever have been photographed. The two marlin at the left were caught from the cruiser Pilar by Ernest Hemingway, author and sportsman, who stands at the extreme left. Next to Mr. Hemingway are Capt. Archie Cass and Carlos, Cuban mate on the Pilar. Mike Lerner stands at the left of his 478-pound marlin, with Capt. Tommy Gifford of the cruiser Lady Grace, at the right. To the right of Captain Gifford is Capt. Fred Lister of the cruiser Willow D, owned by Julio Sanchez of Miami Beach, who caught the 382-pound marlin at the extreme right. The picture, visual evidence of the possibilities of big game fishing in Bimini's Gulf Stream, should go far to establish Miami's neighboring island as "the tops" for this type of sport.—Photograph by Erl Roman.

ANGLER'S NOTES by Erl Roman

IF there were ever any doubts about the increasing popularity of the sport of fishing in this area during the summer months, the activity evident this summer should forever dispel them. Just a few years ago Metropolitan Miami's fishing season, so far as any large number of visitors

The sailfish is peculiar. Unlike most other fish, he stuns his prey before consuming it. In other words, he rarely is hooked at the first strike. He is possed with an elongated snout, or rapier-like sword, with which he taps the trolled bait in order to render it helpless. Some

TOMMY KIGHT LEADS CITY LEAGUE HITTING

Dunn Bus Player Continues To Set Pace For Batters With .474 Average

Dunn Bus' Tommy Knight managed to cling to the batting lead in the Miami City Diamondball League last

Bimini fishing was big news when trumpeted by columnist Erl Roman in the Miami Herald *(1935).*

Just south of Bimini was the private island of Cat Cay, a lush 210 acre tropical paradise and home to the Cat Cay International Tuna Tournament. Founded in 1939 and suspended during the war years, this two-week event quickly reestablished itself and began to yield some exceptional catches. As many as five giant bluefin tuna were caught by a single angler in one day, and there were many reports of epic battles between man and fish that the fish eventually won. Following the Tuna Tournament was a four-week marlin tournament which often featured blue marlin in excess of 700 lb. The slightly more distant island of Walker's Cay also reopened to anglers after the war, and the famed Walker's Cay Club resumed operation in February of 1947. Used as a wartime base by the US Navy, Walker's Cay suffered the most disruption of any Bahamian island but was quick to put itself right again. By 1948, all three destinations were in full repair and anglers flocked to the rich waters nearby.

Just as anglers were growing convinced that big-game fishing couldn't get any better, it did.

Lou Wasey relaxing by the massive Cat Cay Tuna Trophy in the island's Kitten Key Bar. Today the trophy resides in the IGFA's E.K. Harry Library in Florida.

CABO BLANCO, PERU

Long charted by European explorers, Cabo Blanco, Peru lies four degrees south of the equator and is among the most westerly points in South America. Awareness of Cabo Blanco's fishing potential began in the mid-1930s with the capture of a 601 lb black marlin by Canadian Thomas Stokes. Over the next several years, a few other intrepid anglers experienced similar success, and by 1940 Michael Lerner was intrigued enough to organize an AMNH expedition to the region. The results were mind-boggling but quickly overshadowed by the specter of war. Nevertheless, post-war excursions by Enrique Pardo of Lima, Alfred C. Glassell Jr. of Houston and Kip Farrington left little doubt that the world's largest marlin were close at hand. To provide sanctuary while pursuing these beasts, the Cabo Blanco Fishing Club was born in May of 1951 and for the first 15 years was home to some of the most remarkable fishing ever seen.

From an oceanographer's perspective, the reason for such copious abundance is clear. The north-flowing Humboldt current and southerly Equatorial current collide just off the Cabo Blanco shoreline, creating a unique offshore confluence that serves as a spectacular mixer for all types of marine ecology. More than 50 years later, Cabo Blanco pioneer Alfred C. Glassell Jr. can still recall watching in astonishment the endless parade of oceanic life. Tuna, striped marlin, and swordfish were commonly taken within 10 miles of shore, and giant black marlin were often hooked within 300 yards of the beach. During the decade of the 1950s, "grander" black marlin weighing over 1,000 lb were caught in every month of the year except February. From the Cabo Blanco Fishing Club's opening in 1951 until its decline in the late 1960s, there was simply no place else like it on earth.

An aerial view of Cabo Blanco.

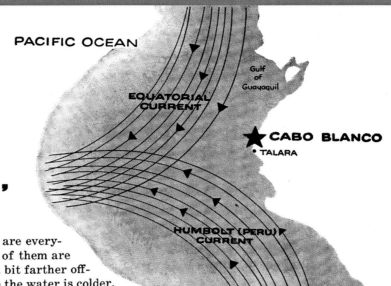

FISHING"

Swordfish are everywhere. Most of them are likely to be a bit farther offshore, where the water is colder.

Dolphin are found anywhere off Cabo Blanco, as are Pacific sailfish, big-eyed tuna and Mako sharks. Roosterfish are taken close to the beach, although the largest are picked up offshore. The wonderful fishing for big amberjack, grouper and smaller species is directly on-shore. No fish of any kind hooked or boated at Cabo Blanco has ever been bitten or mutilated by a shark or any other fish. Surprisingly few sharks are on these fabulous grounds.

Year-Round Angling Season

These waters are the only ones in the world which have a 12-month fishing season.

Both black marlin and broadbill swordfish are taken the year around, in each month. Striped marlin have been caught in 10 different months. Big-eyed tuna, striped marlin, Pacific sailfish, black marlin and swordfish are most numerous from October through June. During the Peruvian winter (the North American summer), the angler can concentrate on black marlin and swordfish, which are most numerous then.

Phases of the moon and the tides apparently have no bearing on the fishing at Cabo Blanco,

Water temperatures fluctuate considerably along the beach from day to day. The best fishing is to be had when there is a good current from the north. This is the normal flow. If the water is not clear, the fish will not show. Some wind is also needed, to keep the black marlin on top.

The only adverse condition is produced by heavy rains, which are rare in northern Peru, occuring only once in many years, or by dirty water flowing into the ocean from rivers swollen by heavy rains in Ecuador.

An important factor in this unique concentration of game fish is, of course, the feed, borne to these waters in abund-

7

As illustrated in this Cabo Blanco Fishing Club yearbook, the collision of the Equatorial and Humboldt currents created a unique environment for anglers.

The Cabo Blanco Fishing Club (1951-1969).

As if the incredible profusion of game fish weren't enough, the waters surrounding Peru's "White Cape" were blessed in other ways as well. While high offshore winds are typical during the latter half of the year, the first six calendar months off Cabo Blanco are characterized by calm winds and flat seas. Heavy rain and the resultant run-off is rare and, except for those times, the water offshore is crystal clear. During the early years, vast bait schools were everywhere, and most major gamefish species were available year-round. Unlike Wedgeport, the weather was usually balmy in Cabo Blanco, and game fish were abundant in both quality and variety. Incredibly (and although rarely pursued), inshore fishing was equally as good. Unlike Bimini, sharks were never a problem and the mutilation of hooked fish by sharks was virtually unheard of. In addition, there was little need for hours of endless trolling, since virtually all billfish species were commonly seen on the surface. Here again, the only problem was accommodations, and the founding of the Cabo Blanco Fishing Club took care of that.

Conceived in the late 1940s as early post-war anglers enjoyed stupendous results, the Cabo Blanco Fishing Club was originally incorporated in Peru by 10 founding members, including Kip Farrington, Alfred C. Glassell Jr., and Peruvian sportsman Enrique Pardo. In all, seven Americans, one Brazilian, one Argentinean, and one Peruvian invested $10,000 apiece in the idea, and club membership would never exceed more than a few dozen of the world's most fortunate anglers. Club facilities consisted of two low-slung clubhouses built on land leased from the Lobitos Oil Company.[5] The first, accommodating 12 guests in remarkable comfort, was opened in 1953 and the second (with rooms for 20) opened a year later. Nominally open to the public, it was primarily a playground for Club members and their guests, and the Club roster read like a *New York Times* society column. Names like DuPont, Firestone, Hulman, and Hutton were among the most recognizable, and a more august list of big-game anglers could scarcely be imagined.

---

[5] *In 1957, Lobitos was acquired by the International Petroleum Company which continued to serve as the Club's landlord and host.*

Never the easiest place to get to, Cabo Blanco was nonetheless usually worth the effort.

Beginning in 1951, Farrington, Glassell and other Cabo Blanco Fishing Club members enjoyed an incredible period of big-game angling that will never be duplicated. Within four years of the Club's opening, 29 members of the Cabo Blanco One-Thousand Pound Club had already been anointed,[6] and 10 world records had been set. Indeed, throughout the Club's history, records of black marlin, striped marlin, swordfish, Pacific sailfish, Allison tuna, bigeye tuna, and other game fish fell with astounding frequency, and the fish stories recounted in many of Farrington's books are hard to imagine today. During that same period, Panama and Ecuador also developed reputations for superb fishing,[7] but neither country could offer the consistent opportunities for giant fish that were just offshore at Cabo Blanco.

To be sure, Cabo Blanco was not for everyone. Aside from the difficulty and expense of getting there (via Lima or Talara), Club rates reflected the logistical nightmare of running such a remote operation. Lodging was $25-$35 per day, and Club boats were available for charter at daily rates between $100 and $125, not inconsiderable sums for the period. Tackle, hotel transport, and service fees were additional. Nevertheless, the accommodations were more than comfortable, and a first-class kitchen provided excellent dining. For the ladies, there were such distractions as swimming, sightseeing, birdwatching and accompanied trips to nearby towns. For the men (and the occasional lady), there was fishing...and what fishing it was!

112

---

[6]*Including four women.*
[7]*In particular, Panama's black marlin fishing and Ecuador's swordfishing were exceptional.*

The Club's interior was comfortable and accommodating to many of the world's leading anglers.

Before the Cabo Blanco Fishing Club had its own boats, anglers fished aboard local boats like this one rigged with outriggers and fighting chairs.

By the end of 1951, the Club already had three boats in operation, and the records began to fall almost at once. Clearly, it was just a matter of time before someone accomplished the magic of boating the first 1,000 lb marlin, and the honor fell to Alfred C. Glassell Jr. in April of 1952. His record 1,025 lb black marlin stood for only four months when it was beaten by Tom Bates' 1,060 lb giant in August. From there, the record escalated until Glassell's legendary capture of a 1,560 lb black marlin in August of 1953, an awe-inspiring record that still stands to this day. In addition to the 38 "grander" black marlin caught in the Club's first dozen years of operation, other vaunted game fish such as swordfish and giant bigeye tuna were taken in consistent numbers. Just as Mike Lerner had discovered more than a decade before, striped marlin were so abundant as to be considered a nuisance and were rarely fished. In the four years between 1959-1963, a total of 66 black marlin, 52 swordfish, and 13 tuna over 200 lb were landed by Club members and guests, all fishing from just four Cape Island-style boats. An invitation to fish Cabo Blanco was a once-in-a-lifetime opportunity not to be missed.

CABO BLANCO FISHING CLUB
CABO BLANCO, PERU

U. S. ADDRESS ... 370 PARK AVE., NEW YORK CITY

APT. 595 - LIMA - PERU

ENRIQUE PARDO
PRESIDENT

21st November, 1960

Mr. William K. Carpenter
President of the International Game Fish Association
Alfred 1 Dupont Building
Miami 32
FLORIDA

Dear Mr. Carpenter:

Please accept our most sincere congratulations on being named
President of such an important Association.

Sincerely yours

Enrique Pardo

5628

CABO BLANCO FISHING CLUB

Cabo Blanco, Peru

(Above) Letter dated November 21, 1960 from Club President Enrique Pardo to Bill Carpenter congratulatiing him on his appointment as IGFA President. (Left) The Cabo Blanco Fishing Club's 1959 yearbook.

Regrettably, no paradise lasts forever, and this one finally ran its course. By 1968, fishing was in decline and a military coup in Peru made domestic travel more difficult. In the year that followed, a new policy of nationalization by the ruling junta kept most American visitors away, and the Cabo Blanco Fishing Club was forced to close shortly thereafter. A later effort at revival proved unsuccessful, and today the Cabo Blanco Fishing Club is a warm but distant memory for its few surviving members. Many early IGFA principals passed through the Club either as members or guests, including IGFA founder Mike Lerner and future IGFA Presidents Bill Carpenter and Elwood Harry. To the Club's everlasting credit, their application of IGFA rules was unforgiving even in such a remote outpost, and the resulting stature of records set there has never been questioned.

By the early 1970s, these three great fisheries were eclipsed by the discovery of colossal black marlin off northeastern Australia. The sensational fishing around Cairns was discovered during WWII but was fished inconsistently and with great logistical difficulty until the early 1960s. Pioneered by American George Bransford, the first "grander" black marlin (1,064 lb) was finally taken there by Richard Obach in 1966, and the region exploded in popularity. Nevertheless, while the world may never again see world records fall as they once did in Bimini, Wedgeport and Cabo Blanco, the sportsmanship and rigor with which those great catches were made will always be among big-game angling's most enduring laurels.

Captain George Bransford (left) and Richard Obach with their ground-breaking 1,064 lb black marlin taken off Cairns, Australia (September 25, 1966).

Sportfishing boats fan out after a shotgun start at the legendary Masters Angling Tournament in Palm Beach, Florida. Founded in 1961, the Masters remains one of the world's most prestigious big-game fishing events.

Chapter Six

THE BILL CARPENTER ERA

With Mike Lerner firmly at the helm, the IGFA welcomed in the post-war era with a flurry of activity. By 1948, the organization had its own phone number and cable address, and the list of countries in which the IGFA could boast of representation was up to 36. As fishing clubs around the world emerged from wartime dormancy, the number of affiliated clubs also increased markedly to 80. For his tireless efforts, Philip Wylie was elevated to First Vice President and selected to head a new Editorial Committee consisting of Francesca LaMonte, AMNH scientist John T. Nichols, and himself. A new record subdivision was established in the area of plugcasting, and for the first time the IGFA began to recognize nylon and synthetic fishing lines for world record consideration. It was an auspicious start, and more was on the way.

Two years later in 1950, the IGFA published its first post-war summary of changes to its organizational structure and rules. By this time, Helen and Mike Lerner had virtually ceased fishing in favor of expending their efforts on the Lerner Marine Laboratory in Bimini. Since his series of pre-war expeditions, Mike had become entranced with marine science and scientists, forging a strong friendship with William Gregory and engaging in many late-night conversations with him on scientific theory and the quest for knowledge.

With the Lerner Lab open and underway in 1948, Mike needed to enlist some new blood to help with the IGFA. He brought in B. Davis ("Bud") Crowninshield, a most accomplished sportsman, Sharp Cup veteran, and pioneering Massachusetts angler, as Vice President and Tackle Committee Chairman and added a new "Associate" category to represent the United States on the International Committee.[1] The first Associates were *Miami*

[1] *Until the creation of the "Associate" position, the IGFA's Executive Committee had served as America's de-facto Representative on the International Committee. A few years later, the Associate post was abolished in favor of direct U.S. Representatives.*

Herald columnist Erl Roman on the East Coast, Dr. George Chuck representing the heartland, and ex-Tuna Club President Joe Peeler serving the western seaboard. All were valuable additions and did much to ease Lerner's burden.

Indeed, there was a lot to do. The IGFA roster had grown tremendously in the two years since its 1948 yearbook. The number of affiliated scientific institutions was now up to 12, and more than 200 angling clubs throughout the world had joined the IGFA and adopted its ideals. Another critical change made in 1949 was the abandonment for record-keeping purposes of linen line thread counts in favor of measured breaking strength. Thus, instead of the previously used 6-, 9-, 15-, 24-, 39-, and 54-thread record categories, new classifications were established for 12-lb, 20-lb, 30-lb, 50-lb, 80-lb, 130-lb, 180-lb, and all-tackle line classes. Not only did this create many new openings for world records,[2] but it gave record opportunities to countless anglers who were unfamiliar with or disliked the high-maintenance nature of linen line. With this important change, new record applications began to accelerate.

---

[2] *In that the six previous line classes had now been replaced by eight.*

119

Caliban at the dock after a good day's fishing.

Things continued apace during the first half of the 1950s. In 1953, the IGFA finally developed a set of bylaws to codify organizational direction and allow for growth. A Board of Governors was split off from the IGFA's Executive Committee to administer the bylaws, and many long-overdue housekeeping matters were resolved. New rules were also adopted on the use of weighmasters, inshore tackle, and procedures for submitting catches for world record consideration. Despite the changes, the IGFA rolled along; one year later the number of affiliated clubs was up to 300 and IGFA Representatives could be found in more than 50 regions around the world. By 1958, the organization had outgrown its AMNH offices and relocated to Florida to be nearer Lerner's Miami home and beloved Bimini laboratory. In conjunction with the move, a number of new IGFA Governors and members of the Executive Committee[3] were added, and the organization appeared poised and ready for another decade of growth. So it was, but it was to be under a new leader.

---

[3] Including boxer-turned-sportsman Gene Tunney.

Angler Gene Tunney (left in photo) with a knock-out tuna taken off Bimini in 1947. Michael Lerner is at right.

International Game Fish Association

affiliated with

THE AMERICAN MUSEUM OF NATURAL HISTORY

ALFRED I. DuPONT BUILDING

MIAMI 32. FLORIDA

RELEASE

June 25, 1960

RELEASED FOR ___PUBLICATION --- JULY 1, 1960

Mr. William K. Carpenter, renowned big game sports fisherman has been elected President of the International Game Fish Association, it was announced today by the Governors of that body. He succeeds Mr. Michael Lerner who has held the IGFA Presidency since 1944, and who now becomes Founder-Chairman of the IGFA.

"I know of no better man for the active job of President of the Association than Bill Carpenter," Mr. Lerner observed today. "He is known by sportsmen, boatmen, guides and anglers from Alaska to the Bahamas and from Nova Scotia to Peru, and in many other lands where deep-sea fishing is a major sport. The IGFA Governors and Executive Committee Members unanimously join me in saluting Bill Carpenter as our new President."

Mr. Carpenter, a resident of Fort Lauderdale, Florida, has been a member of several of the United States Tuna Teams competing in the annual tourney at Wedgeport, Nova Scotia. He captained the 1954 U. S. Team. He holds one of the most remarkable records among anglers — one that it is unlikely will ever be equaled — that of winning six out of eight Cat Cay Tournaments he entered. Those heavyweight battles-royal attract the best and most tireless angler-experts from many nations each Spring.

The IGFA, founded 21 years ago by Mike Lerner at the urging of sportsmen throughout the world, was established for the purpose of drawing up a set of rules for fair and ethical angling, and as a world record keeping organization to maintain records of fish caught in compliance with the established rules. The Rules themselves, as well as all succeeding rule changes, have been voted on by the over 500 Member Clubs and 100 International Representatives located in practically every country of the free world.

Press release dated June 25, 1960 announcing the election of William K. Carpenter as President of the IGFA, succeeding Michael Lerner.

121

In his prime, William K. DuPont Carpenter was a large imposing man of great character and privilege. Heir to the DuPont fortune, Carpenter stood 6'3" and weighed 220 lb, yet he managed to squeeze into cockpits long enough to forge a distinguished career as an Air Force pilot during WWII. He was an avid hunter and sportsman all his life and is widely regarded today as one of the preeminent giant bluefin tuna anglers of all time. Appointed IGFA Vice President in October of 1959, he replaced Mike Lerner as President barely nine months later, a strikingly rapid ascension that was most likely pre-ordained. With Lerner approaching his 70th birthday, it was time for a successor and Bill Carpenter brought not only a sterling fishing resume but also the bank account necessary to undertake the IGFA's ongoing financial responsibilities. There may have been other candidates to succeed Lerner, but not with Carpenter's combination of credentials.

The United States Tuna Team at the 1952 International Tuna Cup Match (Sharp Cup). Standing (l-r): Tony Hulman, Joe Gale, Maurice Meyer, A.W. Whisnant. Below (l-r): Alfred C. Glassell, Jr., George Bass, Bill Carpenter.

In fact, as a big-game angler, Bill Carpenter had few equals. He fished as a member of the U.S. Tuna Team competing for the Sharp Cup from 1952-1955, captaining the team in 1954 and contributing to its victory the following year. By the time of his appointment to the IGFA Presidency in 1960, Carpenter had already landed more than 300 giant bluefin tuna, including seven in one day. His eventual lifetime total of more than 600 such fish has never been duplicated, and his stunning accomplishment in 1963 of releasing 15 giants in a single day[4] remained unmatched for decades. An early conservationist, most of his career tuna were tagged and released, and various recaptures of his fish over the years[5] added significantly to early knowledge of the bluefin's migratory patterns and growth. If all that wasn't impressive enough, Carpenter was also victorious in seven Cat Cay Invitational Tuna Tournaments (out of 10 attempts) and, as an early member of the Cabo Blanco Fishing Club,[6] was a three-time member of the Cabo Blanco One-Thousand Pound Club for his captures of gigantic black marlin there. Clearly, the man knew how to fish.

---

[4] *After returning to the dock that evening, he commented that he could have taken even more but didn't want to set a record that could never be broken.*

[5] *Including one fish tagged in the Bahamas and recaptured off the coast of Norway.*

[6] *In 1983, a visitor to the by-then derelict club pulled Carpenter's marlin-shaped nameplate from his locker and sent it to him. It now resides in the IGFA Library.*

In addition to his many angling successes, Carpenter also shared Lerner's view on the high ethical standard required to maintain the competitive integrity of big-game fishing. He was especially disgusted by the early Cat Cay practice of culling giant tuna out of a school and using the boat to herd a solitary fish into shallow water where quick capture on light tackle was almost assured. He recognized right away that the angler had little to do with such a catch; it was all a matter of skillful boat handling. Finally, he reached the boiling point and prior to the Cat Cay Tournament in 1956 set up a demonstration. Using his boat to separate a large free-swimming bluefin from an offshore school, Carpenter drove it into shallow water where it eventually wallowed from exhaustion and was free-gaffed. This "no-thread" tuna weighed in at 439 lb and soon resulted in the IGFA's banning of such activity.

Carpenter and crew beam alongside his 300th tuna taken in 1959. From left: Chuck Cichowski, George Staros, Carpenter, Allen Merritt.

In a letter to Mike Lerner dated March 18, 1960, Carpenter laid out his thinking on a variety of subjects that almost certainly cemented his appointment as IGFA President later that year. Among other things, he proposed the elimination of chumming or fishing with mammal bait, a technique common to Australia where porpoises and seals were butchered as chum for sharks. The practice had already resulted in some outsized records where enormous sharks had been chummed right to the boat and captured without single line ever leaving the reel. Carpenter also advocated limiting leader length,[7] restricting the breaking strength of leader to twice that of the connected line, and making illegal the practice of herding fish to shallow

---

[7] *He proposed a 15' maximum on heavy tackle and 10' on light.*

124

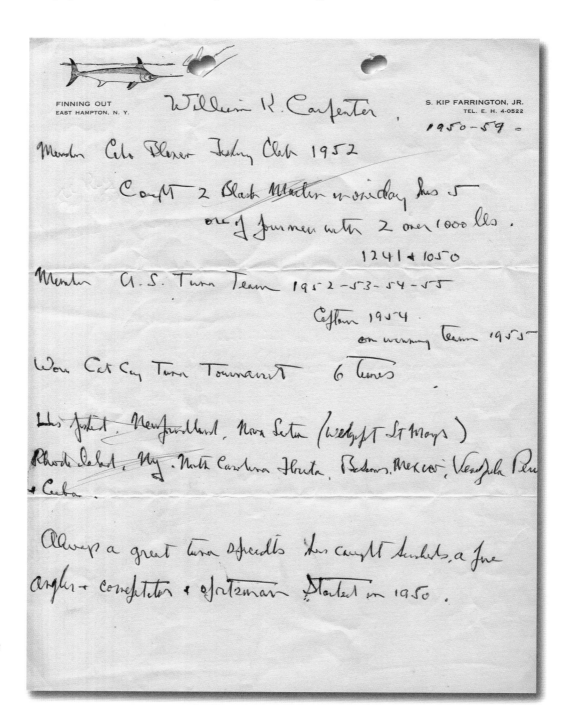

A hand-scribed list of Bill Carpenter's fishing accomplishments during the 1950s, written by Kip Farrington.

water when angling from a boat. He was also not afraid to weigh in against prevailing sentiment, as he did when he argued against the outlawing of flying gaffs. Lerner felt that flying gaffs were too dangerous and conveyed an unfair advantage to the angler. Ultimately, a compromise was reached: the use of flying gaffs remained legal but the length of attached rope was restricted to 30'.

By 1961, saltwater angling was thoroughly in vogue. In April, the sport was featured on the cover of *Life* magazine, and Lerner and Carpenter were extensively profiled. While Lerner did little fishing by that time, Carpenter fished extensively throughout the decade from his well-known game boats *Caliban* and later *Hadit*. Both boats were state-of-the-art, incorporating such recent innovations as tuna towers, rocket launchers and greatly increased speed. Carpenter's 97' yacht *Titian* often served as a mothership to the smaller vessels, and Carpenter's long-time skippers Alan Merritt and later George Staros became angling personalities themselves. Merritt ultimately left Carpenter's employ to rejoin the family boat-building firm, while Staros (with help from his brother Bill) served as Carpenter's personal skipper for more than 30 years.

Saltwater fishing was the cover story in this 1961 issue of Life *magazine.*

In 1964, Carpenter presided over one of the more fascinating meetings held during his tenure, this one having to do with the ephemeral "silver" marlin. In a lengthy letter to Carpenter dated January 21, 1964, Francesca LaMonte expressed her frustration at the continuing presence of silver marlin as an IGFA record category. First identified and named in 1935 by LaMonte and fellow AMNH ichthyologist and IGFA officer John Nichols, the only original evidence of its existence was a rather poor vintage photograph taken in Tahiti. Later photographs of a similar ashen-colored fish taken in Mexico seemed to confirm their original thinking, but by 1958 marine science had come around to regarding the silver marlin as simply a sub-species of black marlin. Nevertheless, IGFA records continued to include silver marlin up through 1964, and LaMonte was offended and embarrassed by this ichthyological lapse.[8]

125

---

[8] *Especially given her brief paper published in 1958 that retracted the initial classification and her continuing position as IGFA Secretary. Indeed, she went to far as to advocate the removal of all scientific names from IGFA records based on a worldwide lack of scientists able to distinguish one related species from another.*

Zane Grey was convinced of the existence of "silver" marlin and held various early records for same. This one (actually a black marlin) was taken in Tahiti in 1930.

Grey's elaborate affidavit verifying his Tahitian catch.

In 1967, Carpenter stepped up his attack on tackle innovations that he considered unfair. When premium Florida reel-maker Fin-Nor released a double-handled reel that conveyed a new degree of leverage to the angler, it was promptly banned. Mechanically-assisted reels, such as those with a ratcheting device, were likewise prohibited. Baits or lures presented with dangling hooks were disallowed on the basis that they fostered snagging; new rules required all hooks to be imbedded in or attached to the bait. Carpenter was also growing concerned about the submission of mutilated fish for record consideration, as it was often impossible to determine the origin of the damage or at what point during the fight it had occurred. Rather than risk inconsistency on a case-by-case basis, the IGFA boldly declared that fish mutilated in any manner were ineligible for world record consideration. While not everyone agreed with this ruling, no one could fault the IGFA for maintaining a clearly understood standard.

Three generations of IGFA Presidents: Michael Lerner, William Carpenter, and Elwood Harry.

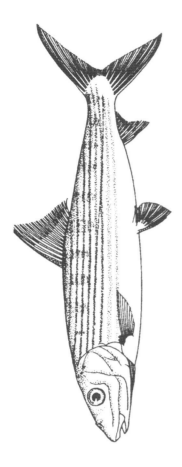

Occasionally, excitement evolved from an unexpected quarter. In December of 1969, the IGFA was indirectly involved in a defamation-of-character lawsuit when a female angler was thrown out of the Islamorada Bonefish Tournament due to a rules infraction. Witnesses indicated that she allowed a guide to cast her bait to a waiting bonefish, but she disputed this accounting by arguing that the guide was merely clearing her tangled line. In the event, her offended husband subsequently filed suit against the tournament organizers and contacted the IGFA for clarification of the appropriate rules. Regrettably, IGFA files are silent as to how this matter was finally resolved.

By 1970, Carpenter had been at the IGFA helm for a decade, and he must have looked back with pleasant satisfaction on his first 10 years. The organization's permanent staff now numbered five people, and membership was continuing to grow. At decade's end, the IGFA roster consisted of 81 Representatives in 43 different regions, 24 member scientific institutions, and 802 member clubs. Mike Lerner still cast a large shadow, but Lerner was aging and had been immersed in the construction of a much larger laboratory on Bimini. Thus, Carpenter was able to press on relatively unfettered with running the organization as he saw fit. He was an able if uninspiring custodian, fortunate to oversee a period of unprecedented growth both in recreational angling and IGFA membership. Nevertheless, Bill Carpenter's legacy improved substantially during the next five years as he set the tone for much of what the IGFA is today.

You are cordially invited to join the International Game Fish Association

Annual dues were $10 for the first individual IGFA members.

Bill Carpenter battles another giant bluefin on Caliban *(ca. 1960). A dozen years later, this fishery was in serious trouble.*

One of Carpenter's most significant contributions was his revamping of the IGFA's desultory publications. Other than its oversized and distinctive world record charts distributed yearly to marinas, tackle stores, and the like, the IGFA had released little new literature since its yearbook in 1948. Mike Lerner had reduced the size of the record charts to pamphlet form in 1956, but there was no accompanying editorial or information. While angling rules had been clearly spelled out by that time, the process of applying for world records was still largely unknown to the average angler.[9] Finally in 1971, the IGFA released its first edition of *World Record Marine Fishes*,[10] a 22-page booklet that included a listing of IGFA officers and member organizations, procedures for submitting record claims, and an up-to-date review of angling rules. Interestingly, in addition to the usual listing of records, it also included a curious selection of records entitled "Lines Not Tested", an apparent catch-all for noteworthy captures that were either inherited from *Field & Stream* or never adjudicated by the IGFA.[11] This category was phased out in 1978 and never appeared again.

129

WORLD RECORD MARINE FISHES

CHARTS

RULES

APPLICATION BLANK

1971

INTERNATIONAL GAME FISH ASSOCIATION

3000 E. Las Olas Boulevard
Fort Lauderdale, Florida 33316, U.S.A.

[9] *Also unknown to most anglers was that while* Field & Stream *magazine continued to maintain the freshwater records, no consideration was given to line class and those were kept only on an all-tackle basis.*

[10] *Later changed in 1979 to* World Record Game Fishes.

[11] *Both LaMonte and Lerner were unhappy to see these records disappear, since many were taken on linen line that was perfectly acceptable in its day. Their position was that if the linen thread count was known, the record was valid.*

By the early 1970s, there were few opportunities for anglers to enjoy this kind of success.

By 1973, Carpenter had begun to think seriously about the IGFA's role in marine conservation. While he himself declined conservation-related advisory positions with the excuse that participating in such would conflict with his obligations to the IGFA, he probably did much to nudge his successor Elwood Harry in that direction. Harry, an accomplished tuna fisherman like Carpenter, joined the IGFA in 1962 as Vice President and is widely credited for much of what occurred under Carpenter's watch. His turn as IGFA President would come in 1975, but until then it was Carpenter's name at the top of the IGFA letterhead. Nevertheless, much (if not most) of what transpired during the early 1970s must be attributable to Harry's vision rather than Carpenter's.

What is unequivocal during this time is that Carpenter (and Harry) were preparing for a major repositioning of the IGFA. In 1973, Carpenter laid out their vision in an open letter to members. Utilizing the annual *World Record Marine Fishes* publication as an editorial platform for the first time, Carpenter noted a lack of centralized communication among marine anglers and dedicated the IGFA to filling that void. He also identified marine conservation as a future platform and vowed to increase the IGFA's efforts in that regard. To finance these initiatives, a new series of individual and corporate memberships were introduced. Finally, member clubs were asked to submit a $25 annual stipend to help defray the cost of these new activities. The gauntlet was down and a new era of IGFA activism had begun.

With conservation now firmly on the agenda, the IGFA was unexpectedly moved to act. When all the numbers were in for 1973, it suddenly appeared that the Atlantic bluefin tuna fishery was in trouble. Both sport and commercial catch statistics were in decline, and many regions along the Atlantic coast were already seriously depleted. In particular, few medium-sized bluefin were being caught, indicating a gross over-exploitation of juvenile fish. Banned from commercial fishing for bluefin in the Gulf of St. Lawrence, Japanese fishing interests had begun to purchase fresh bluefin at premium prices[12] right from the docks, quickly icing the fish and shipping them by air to waiting fish markets in Japan. The potential for financial windfall attracted dozens of new boats with little interest in angling ethics. The result was a dramatic increase in fishing pressure and a huge jump in giant tuna captures from 484 in 1972 to 659 in 1973. These giant fish were the broodstock adults for the entire western Atlantic population, and their numbers were being rapidly diminished.

131

---

[12] At the time, dockside prices for fresh-caught fish were in excess of $2 per pound.

New IGFA flyers began to trumpet the conservation message.

Recognizing this, the IGFA came out swinging in early 1974. Many of the IGFA's senior officers and trustees had spent countless hours in pursuit of these fish, and the imminent collapse of the entire fishery was too painful to consider. As a result, the organization spearheaded a late-1973 conference that called for a much more aggressive fisheries management plan by the International Commission for the Conservation of Atlantic Tunas (ICCAT). The IGFA also initiated domestic lobbying efforts to press its case and began a dialogue with the National Marine Fisheries Service (NMFS) in support of new research. IGFA members were urged to contact their legislative representatives concerning the issue, and studies were undertaken as to the financial impact of recreational angling in various areas. For the first time, the IGFA was galvanized into action in a matter of conservation, and it would set the tone for all future organizational priorities.

Although the progress with governmental agencies was painfully slow, the results elsewhere were encouraging. For the first time since its inception in 1939, the Cat Cay Tuna Tournament went to a tag-and-release format, and all but two of the 24 fish subsequently taken during the event were released. In addition, a number of other eastern seaboard tuna competitions were either scaled back or cancelled, including the 32-year old United States Atlantic Tuna Tournament based in Gloucester, Massachusetts.[13] This was a heartening development, and the IGFA continued to press its case by issuing a resolution in favor of continuing bluefin conservation efforts. With a subject so near and dear to its heart, the organization was finding its voice.

In conjunction with the change to an open membership, Carpenter's next effort at improving the IGFA's lines of communication was even more impressive. A bimonthly newsletter entitled *International Marine Angler*[14] was begun in 1973, a publication that continues to this day. The first *IMA* was a modest eight-

Caliban heads seaward again.

[13] Although Canada's Sharp Cup continued as usual.

Cover of the first International Marine Angler published in 1973.

page effort curiously marked Volume 35, Number 1. The flyer trumpeted the IGFA's change to a membership-based association, outlined the IGFA's goals and policies, and made a number of significant announcements. The introduction of a new 6-lb record line class was heralded, and an eight-paragraph history outlined the IGFA's origins. Part outreach to the angling public and part newsletter to existing club and scientific members, the two-color mailer was a credible first effort in expanding the organization's reach.

From its inception, the *International Marine Angler* was a fountain of information. By issue Number 2 (July/August 1973), the publication was up to 12 pages and the new 6-lb record category was headline news. More than one-half of all record applications received during the year were for the new line class, with some 40% of the overall total submitted by women. Readers also learned of the capture in 1970 of an enormous 1,805 lb blue marlin taken off Hawaii,[15] the passing of noted outdoor author Joe Brooks, and a history of the black marlin fishery unfolding in Cairns, Australia. This last article was written by Daphne Nielsen, one of the IGFA's first women Representatives, and detailed American George Bransford's pioneering efforts off Cairns aboard the legendary game boat *Sea Baby 1*.

---

[14]Later changed to International Angler *after the IGFA assumed responsibility for freshwater record-keeping from* Field & Stream *magazine in 1978.*

[15]*Unavailable for record consideration due to the fact that several different anglers battled the fish.*

The completely redesigned
World Record
Marine Fishes
publication released in
1974.

In 1974, Carpenter presided over yet another dramatic upgrade to the IGFA's public persona with the introduction of a completely redesigned *World Record Marine Fishes* publication. The new book was about half the size of its predecessors but included almost four times the number of pages. World records were now listed by species, and a full page was given over to each one. Thus, all records for the species *Elagatis bipinnulata* (rainbow runner) appeared together, divided only by line class and angler gender. Now more than 30 years later, the IGFA still utilizes this same format for all its record listings.

As 1974 drew to a close, an angling milestone was set when the first catch of an IGFA-compliant 1,000 lb marlin in the Atlantic was confirmed.[16] Others had been reported taken by commercial and subsistence fishermen over the years, but they were rare and documentation was sketchy. However, angler Jack Herrington's capture of an 1,142 lb Atlantic blue marlin off Oregon Inlet (North Carolina) finally laid the issue to rest. A novice billfisherman, Herrington battled the monster marlin for nearly three hours, and seven men were finally required to bring the fish over the boat's transom. Hooked on a squid and 100-lb test line, the catch outweighed the previous IGFA all-tackle record by nearly 300 lb.

[16] *All previous billfish "granders" had come from the Pacific.*

Despite his lack of celebrity today, William K. Carpenter was a man of considerable vision and did much to modernize the IGFA. Continuing ill health during the early 1970s finally forced his resignation from the IGFA Presidency, although he continued as Board Chairman until his death. His successor in 1975 was Elwood Harry, a man of unsurpassed vision and energy who would finish much of what was begun under Carpenter. Nevertheless, Carpenter's expansion of the IGFA's objectives to include marine conservation was most foresighted, and the membership scheme he outlined remains little changed today. Widely honored by prominent members of the sporting community during his latter years, Carpenter was probably most pleased by the naming of a new amberjack species *Seriola carpenteri* by his friend Frank Mather in 1972. Bill Carpenter — sportsman, philanthropist, IGFA visionary - died at his home in Boca Raton in 1987. He was 68.

Jack Herrington's 1,142 lb Atlantic blue marlin taken in 1974 off Nags Head, NC, the first grander billfish ever taken to IGFA specifications in the Atlantic.

Elwood Harry works on his tackle off Nova Scotia.

Chapter Seven

ELWOOD HARRY

From the beginning, Elwood K. Harry lived to fish. A child of the Great Depression, Harry was born April 18, 1914 in E. Petersburg, Pennsylvania to middle-class parents. He was a good student and dutiful son when he wasn't prowling the fertile waterways of the Northeast, catching trout and panfish in a practiced manner that Tom Sawyer would have envied. He came of age in the 1930s well aware of hardship, but his grocery store-owning father was a good provider and Elwood was not unmindful in helping to keep the family business afloat. As he grew into manhood, Harry also expanded his fishing horizons, discovering for the first time the bounty of the eastern seaboard and the rich waters of Chesapeake Bay. In May of 1938, he married his sweetheart Adele ("Teddy") Eby and prepared for a conventional life.

However, World War II changed all that. Somewhat by accident, Harry fell into an aircraft consultancy position with the USAAF during the war and along the way developed a considerable expertise in aviation logistics and supply. WWII was the first great air war in which planes were used by both sides in copious numbers. However, the art of keeping large numbers of aircraft in the air was a relatively new one, requiring a proprietary supply pipeline and special infrastructure unknown to previous conflicts. It was a brand new field, and in it Elwood Harry found his life's work. At the war's conclusion, he opened his own business in aviation supply and was soon a successful part of the post-war aviation boom. By 1950, he was well on his way to becoming a made man, and it had become time to stoke his lifelong passion for fishing.

Already an accomplished freshwater angler, Harry's growing financial means allowed him to expand his angling horizons and he soon fell in love with the burgeoning sport of giant tuna fishing. Over the course of a widely-traveled angling career, Harry caught more than 600 giant bluefin tuna, an astounding record and perhaps second only to Bill Carpenter's all-time mark. A keenly competitive angler, Harry captained the United States team during many years of the Bahamian International Tuna Competition, and he competed (and often won) as a U.S. team member in the Sharp Cup matches off Nova Scotia. For the 20-year period between 1950 and 1970, there were few anglers anywhere in the world more successful in catching giant bluefin tuna than Elwood Harry.

A young Harry works away at his desk (ca. 1950).

Elwood went wherever the
tuna were. This catch was
made in Cabo Blanco, Peru
in 1958.

    Having discovered the warm and captivating Cat Cay in 1954, Harry
found his tournament stride in 1959 when he caught the largest fish[1] at
the Cat Cay Tuna Tournament, finally breaking Bill Carpenter's dominance
of the event. The following year, Harry caught three out of only seven
fish taken during the entire contest, and the Harry legend was underway.[2]
He went on to catch 38 giant bluefin during one 30-day span in 1963,[3] a
monumental feat of endurance that earned him the nickname "Ironhands".
Harry was also famous for his superstitious wearing of bright red socks in
tournament settings, once prompting a local run on red socks by frustrated
anglers looking to emulate his technique.

[1] At 640 lb.

[2] After again capturing the largest tuna during the 1962 tournament, he retired and took home the Aksel
Wichfeld Tuna Trophy for repeating the feat three years in a row. The trophy now resides in the IGFA
library.

[3] The vast majority of which were tagged and released.

Harry with a Cat Cay Tournament catch.

A graceful angler and diligent student of his quarry, Harry's angling style was not so much defined by muscle as it was by preparation. Many anglers were physically stronger, but Harry always came ready for battle and rarely lost a fish due to sloppiness. Four weeks in advance of each new season, he would retreat to his basement gym to get ready. Thus prepared, and with his wife Teddy often watching from high in the boat's tuna tower, he was a master at placing his bait just so that the largest bluefin at the rear of the school would be unable to resist. He loved such fishing and was convinced that the only true game fish worthy of 130-lb test line was the giant bluefin tuna. Despite his success (or perhaps because of it), Harry rarely weighed a fish outside of a tournament setting, and his adherence to a policy of catch-and-release did not go unnoticed by other anglers of the era.

While fishing the Sharp Cup in the 1950s and 1960s,[4] he met and became friendly with IGFA founder Mike Lerner. Many long conversations about the future of big-game angling ensued, and Harry found himself in wholehearted agreement with Lerner and his ideals. In 1962, he was tapped to fill the IGFA Vice Presidential vacancy created by the death of Ernest Hemingway, and seven years later he retired from business to spend

---

[4] *He served as captain of the U.S. team in 1968.*

more time on organizational initiatives. In the interim, he learned much from Carpenter and Lerner, often standing in for one or both during their frequent absences to lend a steady hand. As the 1960s drew to a close, Harry could see the IGFA's bright future and especially how it needed to change in order to fulfill its potential.

By the early 1970s, Harry had assumed the role of the IGFA's de-facto President, running much of the day-to-day operation and cementing his position as heir-apparent to Bill Carpenter. In a confidential report to the IGFA's Board of Trustees in 1972, he laid out the organization's recent accomplishments and his view of the future. While hardly plush, the new IGFA offices in Fort Lauderdale were a substantial improvement over those in Miami, and Harry recounted that success along with many other recent upgrades to various systems and procedures. Much more oversight was being performed on the granting of records and the actions of International Representatives, and the added rigor had helped reverse a period of inactivity and inattention. Now, Harry felt it was time for the entire organization to grow up. With messianic certainty, he declared that the IGFA should be registered as a nonprofit corporation and that its distinctive insignia be trademarked. More importantly, the heretofore privately-funded organization needed to find a better way of financing itself than dipping into the deep pockets of its Presidents.

141

Hooked up again in the Bahamas.

Harry's report made a telling case that the IGFA's reliance on club memberships was not working. Since establishing their no-cost relationship with the IGFA, nearly one-half of the 650 affiliated clubs had not corresponded with the organization in any way. Only 145 clubs cast votes on the matters presented to them in 1971, and fewer than 70 had voted during the prior year. While some reasons were understandable,[5] the upshot was that the IGFA was reaching fewer and fewer of its constituents. Moreover, as a privately-funded organization, the IGFA had little connection or fealty to the average recreational angler. Instead, Harry's vision called for a global membership-based organization that would serve as the governing body to sportfishing interests around the world. He recognized that membership growth held the key to the IGFA's future success, and Harry sold that idea with a fervor. When the Trustees finally agreed, the stage was set for a modern IGFA to emerge.

---

[5]Many clubs were small with no clubhouse or address, and club officers changed frequently.

142

After Harry would descend from the tuna tower to do battle, his wife Teddy would often watch from the same perch.

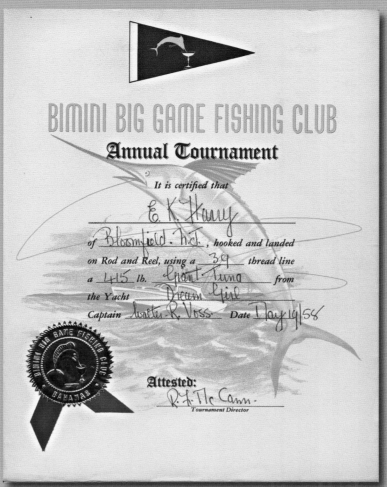

In 1973, the first of Harry's initiatives was put in place. In March, the IGFA was rechartered as a 501(c)(3) nonprofit organization, allowing for donations and contributions to be tax-deductible. Membership was also opened to individuals, and a series of paid membership[6] categories was established. Angling clubs could still belong at no cost but were encouraged to step up to a new $25 "Contributing Club" membership. New corporate memberships, a scholarship fund, and other financial mechanisms were added as well. Recognizing that the IGFA needed to increase its public appeal if it was to attract paying members, a long list of new objectives was also laid out. New efforts in statistical gathering, analysis, tagging support, seminar sponsorship, publication development, grant-making, and education were outlined, a somewhat muddled list but one that accurately reflected Harry's goal of greatly expanding the IGFA's reach. The message did not fall on deaf ears, as within a year more than 2,500 individual memberships had been sold and even club memberships increased to 900. Just as Harry had hoped, the IGFA was on its way to becoming the voice of the marine game fisherman throughout the world.

---

[6] *From Regular ($10 per annum) to Patron ($1,000).*

Elwood Harry receives the Aksel Wichfeld Memorial Trophy at the 1959 Cat Cay Tuna Tournament. The trophy was retired and presented to Harry after his unprecedented third straight win and is now on display at the IGFA's E.K. Harry Library of Fishes in Florida.

During that same time, fishing was in the news for a number of interesting reasons. The 200 mile territorial limit had been adopted by the U.S. Senate in 1974, and angling interests were keenly following the bill's passage. Efforts at protecting the Atlantic bluefin tuna were also underway, and new catch restrictions established by Canada and Japan were heartening.[7] Offsetting this progress was a report released by Japan summarizing their commercial fishing results for 1973. The numbers were staggering: nearly one million billfish and six million tuna had been taken that year by some 402 million hooks. Despite a 2% increase in effort over the previous year, the number of total fish captures actually declined in eight out of 11 reporting categories. The results were printed in the IGFA's *International Marine Angler* without comment, but they needed little.

There was also much to report of regional interest. Among other things, black marlin taken off Australia were found to include unhealthy quantities of mercury, and porpoise kill incidental to the use of commercial purse seines declined to 78,000 individuals in 1976 from 134,000 the previous year. Elsewhere that year, cousins Jerry and Jesse Webb opened Florida's eastern seaboard to night swordfishing with their capture of two swordfish weighing 348 and 368 lb on the night of July 6, 1976. Within a year of the

[7]*Although largely ineffectual.*

Webbs' first recreational catches, dozens of boats were participating in the new fishery and the first Miami Swordfish Tournament was scheduled for the following year. Although longlining at night for Florida swordfish had already been proven, the ability of recreational anglers to catch swordfish while adrift at night was a new and original idea, just the kind of thing that Elwood Harry enjoyed.

When finally appointed IGFA President in 1975, Harry wasted no time in applying his imprint to the organization he loved. Concerned that so many records had climbed out of reach of the casual angler, Harry inaugurated an Annual Fishing Contest that would become one of the IGFA's most popular award programs. With the slate cleared every year, the IGFA was now able to recognize thousands of exceptional but not record-breaking catches. The following year, Harry introduced the metric system to IGFA record-keeping, and subsequent world record listings would show all line classes and fish weights both in Imperial and metric weights. With more projects in mind than money in hand, he also increased the individual membership dues from $10 to $15 per annum. In a final spate of early-term activity, Harry set about to redesign the IGFA's signature record book in a dramatic way.

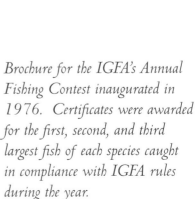

145

Brochure for the IGFA's Annual Fishing Contest inaugurated in 1976. Certificates were awarded for the first, second, and third largest fish of each species caught in compliance with IGFA rules during the year.

In the spring of 1978, IGFA members were stunned when they pulled their annual *World Record Marine Fishes* book from the mailbox. Gone was the undersized format and dry recitation of facts and figures. The new *WRMF* was a 240-page perfect-bound goliath, chockablock with color photographs, advertisements, and editorials written by some of the leading outdoor writers of the day. Each of the now 64 record species had its own page with a detailed line drawing and data on distribution, identifying features, behavior patterns, and more. The cover photo was a spectacular shot of a somersaulting tarpon, a sight to thrill even the most unflappable anglers and a distinctive symbol of the frenetic action underway at IGFA headquarters. Elwood Harry's day had dawned, and he was wasting no time.

Despite a formidable Executive Committee[8] and Board of Trustees, the IGFA was Harry's organization from the beginning. As President, he was a benevolent dictator, listening politely to the Board's suggestions and then proceeding as he saw fit. Totally dedicated, Harry was also persuasive, energetic, and had a wonderful talent for organization. His wife Teddy was pressed into service as a full-time volunteer, and together they spent countless nights and weekends working to expand the IGFA's reach. Notoriously tight-fisted, Harry would clean the office carpets at night and had a penchant for not returning long-distance phone calls so that the caller would have to call back. Nevertheless, Harry grew in confidence as his tenure progressed and was adored by anglers around the world.[9] As evidenced by the many brand-name advertisers in the newly expanded

World Record Marine Fishes, Harry was also roundly backed by the recreational boating and fishing industries, and this further solidified his position.

---

[8] *Including past Presidents Mike Lerner and Bill Carpenter.*
[9] *He was known in the Bahamas and Puerto Rico as "The Pope".*

Harry surprised and delighted the IGFA membership with his redesign of the World Record Marine Fishes *book in 1978.*

Recognizing that fishing organizations worldwide had been slow to adopt the conservation mantle, Harry quickly positioned the IGFA to assume a leadership role. He understood that communication and education were the keys to marshalling support for conservation issues, and he began by trumpeting the conservation message through all of the IGFA mouthpieces at his disposal. Not surprisingly, Harry's first efforts were in support of an initiative to

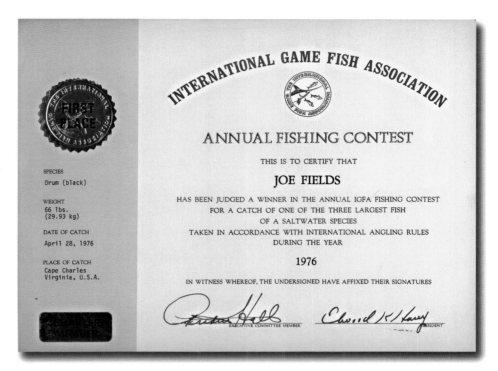

A first place certificate awarded during the IGFA's first Annual Fishing Contest in 1976.

protect his favorite species, the Atlantic bluefin tuna. In a variety of open letters and editorials, Harry pinned blame for declining bluefin stocks squarely on the countries with large longline fleets, especially Russia, Norway and Japan. He noted that recreational anglers annually captured a miniscule number of fish compared to commercial interests and emphasized the highly unproductive nature of fishing with rod and reel. By voicing such strong views, Harry served to push the IGFA into the limelight as the first international champion of recreational angling and became a bona fide hero to big-game fishermen in the process.

One of Harry's most ambitious goals was realized in 1978 when the IGFA absorbed all freshwater world records previously maintained by *Field & Stream* magazine. Keeper of such records since 1910, the magazine saw little benefit in continuing to do so and was delighted when Harry agreed to take on the responsibility along with its considerable effort and expense. Not everyone was thrilled; Mike Lerner was not at all in favor of the IGFA taking on any additional record-keeping duties. In a letter to Harry in December of 1977, Lerner decried the additional expense required to maintain such records and noted the considerable difficulty of verifying to IGFA standards the records already in place. The note was also signed by IGFA icon Francesca LaMonte and undoubtedly put considerable pressure on Harry to reconsider. Nevertheless, Harry never wavered, and the new record-keeping duties were undertaken shortly thereafter.[10]

---

[10] *A few weeks later, Harry responded with a bland note to Lerner thanking him for his thoughts.*

Prior to 1978, world record charts were occasionally published by a variety of organizations and typically credited both *Field & Stream* and the IGFA for their respective maintenance of fresh and saltwater world records. In addition to an annual review in their own publication, *Field & Stream* also published oversized charts for distribution to landings, tackle shops, outdoor writers, and other interested parties. All of the files and correspondence pertaining to such records were now transferred to the IGFA, a not inconsiderable quantity of data in the era before personal computers and database management. Many records were unverified and incomplete, with some dating back to the mid-1800s. Undaunted, Harry took it all.

Later that same year, Harry also accepted record-keeping duties from the Salt Water Fly Rodders of America and the International Spin Fishing Association, a trifecta that would finally consolidate all world record-keeping for recreational angling under one roof. The "Salty Fly Rodders" had maintained saltwater fly records since 1963 and had adhered to generally high standards in the granting of same.[11] After considerable discussion, the spinfishing records were absorbed into the regular freshwater marks, but ISFA files still exist to this day in the IGFA Library archives. All this was accomplished in 1978, and Harry immediately began the massive effort of streamlining three entirely different sets of record-keeping procedures.

---

[11]*Early SWFROA members included such angling luminaries as Stu Apte, Joe Brooks, Harold Gibbs, Lefty Kreh, Mark Sosin, Charles Waterman, and Lee Wulff.*

IGFA President E.K. Harry accepts the handover of freshwater record-keeping duties from Michael J. O'Neill, publisher of Field & Stream *magazine in 1978.*

I.G.F.A. CERTIFICATION

1984 World Angling Conference

We hereby certify that:

MICHAEL, JEANNIE and ARTHUR RIVKIN

is properly registered to attend the International Game Fish Association (I.G.F.A.) First WORLD ANGLING CONFERENCE to be held at Cap D'Agde, France, September 12-18, 1984. All discounts for travel and other services shall be extended to the party.

I.G.F.A. Official

International Game Fish Association

3000 East Las Olas Boulevard
Fort Lauderdale, FL 33316-1616   USA

In 1984, the IGFA held a World Angling Conference in Cap D'Agde, France to discuss the issues facing recreational anglers.

Nevertheless, within a year records and requirements for freshwater and saltwater fly categories were published under the IGFA banner, and a freshwater fly program was established the following season.

Predictably, absorbing these new responsibilities was not without some transitional difficulty. In a letter to then Board Chairman Bill Carpenter in 1982, Harry noted the fact that existing records for freshwater tippet classes (2-lb, 4-lb, 8-lb, 12-lb, and 16-lb) were not the same as those for saltwater (6-lb, 10-lb, 12-lb, and 15-lb). While tackle manufacturers were eager to see the IGFA unify both fresh and saltwater tippet classes for purposes of record-keeping, it proved to be too difficult to do. Additionally, the 10-lb and 12-lb saltwater tippet classes were so close that distinguishing one from the other for purposes of record-granting was almost impossible. As a result, the saltwater tippet classes were separated by 4-lb increments, a decision that ultimately carried over to all record categories. This change prompted an immediate spate of correspondence from disenfranchised record-holders, including one from Eugene DuPont III[12] in favor of his wife Laura's record black marlin caught on 10-lb test line in 1972. Nevertheless, in the highest traditions of the IGFA, Carpenter resisted such family entreaties and Laura's fish disappeared from the record books.

[12]Dated July 28, 1982.

Swordfish bills taken by angler Alfred C. Glassell, Jr. during his celebrated career, now on display at the E.K. Harry Library of Fishes.

In 1980, a final record-keeping consolidation occurred when the Hayward, Wisconsin-based National Fresh Water Fishing Hall of Fame agreed to forego further freshwater world record-keeping efforts and allow the IGFA to serve as the single universal clearinghouse for such information. Hall of Fame executive Bob Kutz noted at the time that his organization wanted to return to emphasizing its display facility featuring an enormous walk-through muskellunge at the front of the building.[13] By year's end, the IGFA had accepted more than 150 new class records and 20 fly records in the freshwater category, eclipsing even the number of saltwater records established during the same period. Finally, some of the promise that Harry had long seen from this quarter was being realized.

Surely one of Harry's most personally satisfying accomplishments during his tenure was the development of a library for fishing-related ephemera and artifacts. The IGFA's International Library of Fishes had been formally started in 1973, and it quickly grew into Harry's pride and joy. Until then, no central clearinghouse of fishing history existed anywhere in the world. Always a grand visionary, Harry saw the complex as ultimately becoming a global database as well as repository, and both goals have since been wonderfully achieved. Once his concept was approved by the IGFA Board, Harry began soliciting book collections from his many contacts and correspondents. Early gifts from Joe Brooks, Bill Carpenter, Kip Farrington, Michael Lerner, and A.J. McClane cornerstoned the collection, and subsequent donations from such personalities as Kay Brodney, Alfred C. Glassell, Jr., Ann Kunkel, Charles Mather, Frank Mather, George Reiger, and Dade Thornton enhanced it further. Harry was ceaseless in promoting the Library and was never shy in asking for donations.

150

[13] *While the National Fresh Water Fishing Hall of Fame later reinstituted national freshwater record-keeping, all state and world freshwater records continue to be maintained by the IGFA.*

This elegant trophy in sterling silver was created by the Panama Insurance Company to recognize the outstanding big-game catch of the year in Panama waters. Presented for only 10 years (1953-1962), it was retired and now resides in the IGFA's E.K. Harry Library in Florida.

As the Library grew, Harry became even more proactive. He would aggressively search out and ask for copies of new books and actively collected even in categories that were only marginally relevant to angling.[14] A pack rat by nature, Harry also bestowed upon the Library much of his own personal accumulation. Indeed, the IGFA archives throughout the Harry era are remarkably intact today, including private correspondence, office memoranda, and much original documentation from the absorption of *Field & Stream* and spinfishing records. His early embrace of technology did much to aid the Library's advancement as well, first in an early indexing of fishing periodicals and later in a massive in-depth subjecting effort not concluded until 1992.

Ultimately renamed the E. K. Harry Library of Fishes and located at the IGFA Fishing Hall of Fame in Florida, Harry's brainchild today includes

---

[14]*For example, postage stamps pertaining to fish.*

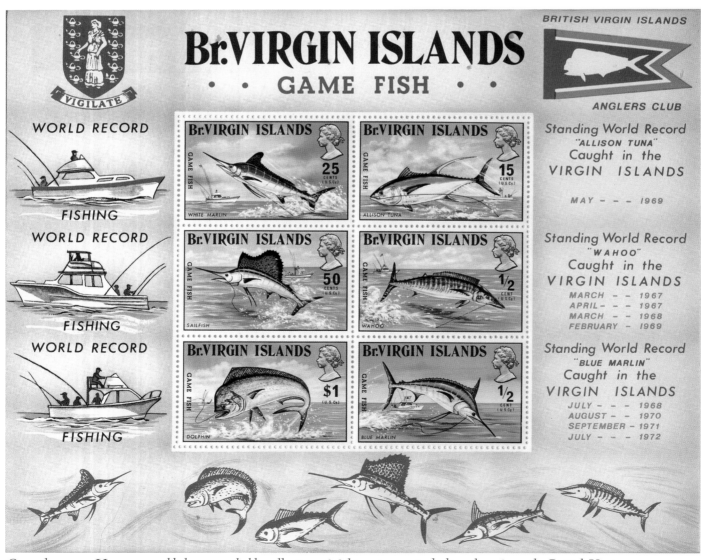

Over the years, Harry assembled a remarkable collection of fishing stamps including these from the British Virgin Islands.

Among Harry's proudest moments was his presiding over the IGFA's 50th anniversary in 1989. This patch was created to celebrate the milestone.

one of the most remarkable single-topic collections in the world. Open to members and non-members alike, its reference collection has grown to include more than 14,000 books dating to 1583, several thousand films and videos from the earliest days of big-game angling, thousands of current and vintage photographs, much original artwork, and various artifacts. The Library regularly receives some 150 magazines and newsletters concerning matters of interest to anglers around the world, and its various collections of fishing-related postage stamps, big-game tournament memorabilia, and vintage angling trophies[15] are unparalleled. Also present is a climate-controlled rare book room where important first editions, early photographs, tackle catalogues, and smaller artifacts are stored. Were he alive today, Elwood Harry would be tickled pink.

In this and all other efforts, Harry maintained a staggering written correspondence throughout his 17-year tenure. Willing to respond in writing to virtually any inquiry, he taxed his long-time secretary Marion McKelvey with the volume. Harry commented on pending legislation, congratulated new world record holders (and commiserated with those whose records had been broken), explained rejected record applications, responded to rule inquiries, corresponded with member clubs, accepted dinner invitations, and discussed fishing itineraries with complete strangers. When he wasn't writing he was traveling, appearing regularly at virtually every big-game angling event around the world and always looking for opportunities to further the sport of big-game fishing.

153

---

[15] *Perhaps the most interesting of which is the massive Cat Cay Tuna Tournament trophy dating to 1939 and first won by legendary Cuban angler Julio Sanchez.*

Teddy and Elwood Harry celebrating a lifetime of achievement.

Despite his equal-opportunity appearances, he did not view all tournaments in an equal light. In particular, Harry was not in favor of money tournaments, often commenting about their failure to promote conservation and notable lack of angling spirit. Just like Hemingway before him, Harry recognized that fishing for money brought out the worst in human nature, and he lamented the loss of good sportsmanship so often seen at these events. Nevertheless, he recognized their appeal and was anxious that the IGFA be as inclusive as possible with its approach to all types of angling. Thus, while the IGFA was regrettably silent in condemning such tournaments,[16] IGFA Representatives were not permitted to participate as judges.

Long-faced and be-jowled in his prime, he became more avuncular in his later years and was deeply revered in sportfishing circles throughout the world. Plagued by health problems towards the end, it was still a shock when he died at age 78 while still IGFA President in June of 1992. Prior to his death, he was honored by leaders in many fields, and he lived long enough to celebrate with his wife Teddy their 54th wedding anniversary. Elwood Harry's contributions to the IGFA were immense and today his name continues to evoke the warmest of memories among anglers and associates around the world. With his passing, a special era of IGFA energy and enthusiasm was stilled.

---

[16] *A position little changed to this day.*

Sword Dance, *the spectacular Kent Ullberg sculpture that adorns the front of the*
IGFA Fishing Hall of Fame & Museum in Dania Beach, Florida.

Chapter Eight

THE MIKE LEECH YEARS

Just as Elwood Harry had stepped into the ailing Bill Carpenter's shoes two decades before, so now did Mike Leech come to Harry's rescue in the early 1990s. Elwood had been suffering from heart trouble for many years, curtailing both his fishing and frenetic travel schedules as a result. By 1983, IGFA Trustees were concerned enough to suggest an assistant to Harry, and Mike Leech was among the first respondents to a subsequent ad placed in the *International Angler.*[1] Harry took to Leech right away, perhaps recognizing in him the same passion for angling and wealth of experiences that Harry saw in himself. Leech's 10 years under Harry and subsequent 10 years as IGFA President were among the most formative of any Presidential tenure, and the range of his contributions cannot be overstated.

157

[1] *Changed from* International Marine Angler *in 1981*

Mike Leech, IGFA's fifth President.

Born in 1935 in Barrington, Rhode Island, Michael Leech was a fisherman almost from birth. His physician father was a heart specialist and recognized the healthy benefits to a vigorous outdoor life. The family always had boats of various sizes, so Leech grew up fishing Narragansett Bay and Cuttyhunk for striped bass as well as the local watering holes for crappie and perch. Upon graduating college with a degree in business, he spent four years in the Coast Guard followed by stints as a real estate developer and stockbroker. Along the way, he met and married his charming wife, Gussie Pace, in 1971.[2] However, by 1976 Leech was ready for a change of pace. Leaving the private sector behind, he spent six formative and successful years as Executive Director of the Florida Council of 100, an economic promotional group based in south Florida. When the chance came to meld his professional expertise with his passion for fishing, Leech was quick to jump at the chance.

---

[2] *They had one son (Eric, born 1978).*

As with all previous IGFA Presidents, Leech was a passionate and extremely capable angler.

THE BREAKERS, PALM BEACH. FLORIDA

INTERNATIONAL GAME FISH ASSOCIATION

45th
Anniversary

Celebration And Auction

Friday
January 11
6 to 11 p.m.

Henry Morrison
Flagler Museum
Palm Beach, Florida

The IGFA's first big fund-raiser in 1984 was held at the Flagler Museum in Palm Beach and proved to be hugely successful. A year later, it was moved to The Breakers, a Palm Beach landmark built by Standard Oil Company magnate Henry Flagler during the early 1900s.

For the first six months after joining the IGFA, Leech was a fixture in Harry's office, watching the maestro at work. When physically sound, Harry was a walking encyclopedia of fishing and at the peak of his formidable personality. Nevertheless, Harry's confidence in Leech grew rapidly and after six months, Mike was on his own. Thereafter, Leech read voraciously to keep up the pace and maintained extensive files on everything from acid rain to sea monsters. Harry also allowed Leech the latitude to develop a number of new programs, the first and most successful of which was a fund-raising dinner hastily thrown together in 1984. Despite Harry's skepticism, the affair was an overwhelming success and went on to become the IGFA's single most productive fund-raising event. Still held annually at The Breakers Hotel in Palm Beach, the evening brings together a dazzling array of anglers and merchandise from around the world.

By early 1992, Harry's health was in marked decline and Leech had assumed many of his day-to-day responsibilities. Promoted some years before to the position of Executive Director, Leech was by then well versed in the organization's many nuances. While Harry's death in June of that year was a shock both to Leech and the IGFA Trustees, the Board quickly convened three weeks later to take up the matter of his successor. Somewhat to Leech's surprise, no Trustee was prepared to assume the Presidential role, so longtime Trustee George Matthews was named to replace Harry as Board Chairman and Leech was appointed the IGFA's fifth President. With an agenda based on experience, Leech went quickly to work.

One of the earliest Rybovich hulls, Miss Chevy IV *was legendary for her sleek lines and greyhound speed.*

Leech's first full year at the IGFA helm (1993) was an eventful one elsewhere as well. In February, an underground bomb rocked the World Trade Center in New York, and two months later a bizarre stand-off in Waco, Texas ended in flames. In the fall, an unprecedented peace agreement between Israel and Egypt was shortly followed by Russian President Boris Yeltsin's brutal suppression of a Soviet hardliners' rebellion. On the waterfront, the angling world was saddened by the death of pioneering boatbuilder John Rybovich who died in Palm Beach at the age of 80. Among many other career accomplishments, Rybovich helped start the legendary Masters Angling Tournament[3] and developed a number of big-game fishing innovations that quickly found their way into offshore cockpits around the world. With such events swirling around him, Leech settled into the IGFA's top spot, still slim and youthful at the age of 58 and ready to assume the oversized mantle of his predecessors. He knew he had a lot to do.

In fact, Leech inherited an organization rich in history but on the verge of becoming marginalized. In the 20 years since the IGFA had become a membership-based association, a relatively modest 16,000 individual members had been added. The majority (75%) were deep-sea anglers based in the U.S. with the rest spread over 90 different countries. Despite Harry's efforts towards creating a compelling membership story, there were few

---

[3]*Originally hosted by the Sailfish Club in Palm Beach; now held annually in Cancun, Mexico.*

tangible benefits to joining other than the annual *World Record Game Fishes* publication. While *WRGF* was a veritable encyclopedia of articles, contacts, and information for the offshore angler, the book included barely a nod to freshwater anglers beyond the basic rules and freshwater records. In fact, the IGFA's longtime focus on big-game angling had made the organization look elitist and unwelcoming to other types of fishermen. Moreover, many records — both fresh and saltwater — appeared unbeatable and unworthy of effort even to the dedicated angler. Leech recognized all that and wasted no time in implementing a flurry of new initiatives.

1992

International Game Fish Association

WORLD RECORD

Freshwater, Saltwater, and Fly Fishing

GAME FISHES

At the beginning of Leech's tenure in 1992, there were few benefits to IGFA membership other than the annual World Record Game Fishes *publication.*

These and other recognition clubs were originated by Leech early in his tenure.

Although membership growth was clearly a priority, the weak bundle of membership benefits and increasing competition from local and regional groups made this a daunting task. Leech launched a multi-pronged attack, adding new types of memberships,[4] establishing a multitude of programs and services and, in a significant break with tradition, introducing IGFA sponsorship to a series of invitational world championship tournaments. Carefully selected regional events created the invitational pool, and all participants were required to hold active IGFA membership. Winners qualified to participate in IGFA-run world championship fish-offs that ultimately included separate inshore, offshore, and junior competitions. Partly as a result, IGFA membership nearly doubled to more than 27,000 members by the year 2000. However, the launching of the Rolex/IGFA Tournament of Champions in 2000 also represented a lamentable departure from Michael Lerner's original vision and was viewed with quiet regret by a few long-lived observers.

In his first Presidential letter to members in the 1993 *WRGF*, Leech sent a clear signal that many new programs would be forthcoming, and he was as good as his word. Line over-testing had long been a contentious source of world record disqualifications, and Leech introduced a line-testing service so that members could assure themselves of line class compliance in advance of their world record pursuits.[5] This was followed by a scale certification program, new membership discounts, introduction of upgraded IGFA-brand apparel and merchandise lines, and the origination of a series of new conservation awards. Leech also added to the IGFA's ability to recognize significant if non-record-breaking catches by promoting its Annual Fishing Contest and creating a series of new achievement-based clubs. Interest was keen, and by the year 2000 membership in 11 such clubs[6] required 16 pages of small print in the annual *WRGF* to list.

---

[4] Including corporate, family, junior and lifetime memberships.
[5] In one test of 25 different lines conducted in 1996, some 40% exceeded their published breaking strength.
[6] Including the Thousand Pound Club, 10 Pound Bass Club, 25 Pound Snook Club, various Grand Slam Clubs and four catch-weight-to-line-class Clubs: 20 to 1, 15 to 1, 10 to 1 and 5 to 1.

OFFSHORE CHAMPIONSHIP

INSHORE CHAMPIONSHIP

On top of these many new IGFA activities and programs, Leech also oversaw a dramatic increase in the number of world record listings. At the beginning of 1993, all-tackle records were kept for 452 different species of fresh and saltwater fish. By 2003, that number had climbed to 832.[7,8] In addition, the decade of the '90s witnessed a tremendous boom in light-tackle fishing as increasing numbers of anglers took to more sporting tackle. In response,[9] Leech oversaw the reintroduction of a 6-lb line class record category previously discontinued in 1982. That by itself opened up hundreds of new record categories, and the vast majority of new marks established during the decade were done so on lighter lines. Indeed, recreational anglers displayed so much enthusiasm for records during this period that entirely new record categories were tossed about: stand-up tackle records, fly tackle records for women, separate records for the new millennium, and even a Tuna Club-sponsored request to recognize catches made on obsolete linen line. Nevertheless, forbearance prevailed and, except for a number of records established for women on saltwater fly tackle, the other proposals ultimately came to naught.

---

[7] Note that full line class records are kept only for a lesser number of actively-pursued species.
[8] As of December 2004, that number had risen to 935.
[9] Also partly in consideration of line manufacturers anxious to establish a new line class record category.

By the early 1990s, the IGFA's original logo had been diluted by various modifications over the years.

Guy Harvey's new logo for the IGFA included both more color and a wider assortment of species.

164

By the decade's midpoint, Leech had the IGFA once again on the move. To better symbolize the organization's new scope, IGFA Trustees finally adopted an updated logo in 1996 after eight years of discussions. Created by noted marine artist (and IGFA Trustee) Guy Harvey, the new artwork included six animated fish in a global domain. A variety of species was chosen to represent the range of IGFA record-keeping, and the look was distinctive and fresh. Ornamented with the colorful new logo, the *International Angler* was also given a makeover and subsequently went to a full-color format two years later. With a more contemporary look now in place, Leech prepared to launch what would become one of the signature initiatives of his tenure: the Junior Angler Program.

Despite the growing demand for an angling program aimed at juniors, the idea was slow to catch on with the IGFA Trustees. Nevertheless, Leech was persistent and after three meetings he finally had their approval to proceed. After considerable planning, the Junior Angler Program was launched in January of 1997 to widespread acclaim. The Program's centerpiece was an entirely new world record category for juniors featuring 100 junior world record species.[10] Four divisions were established, including "Small Fry" divisions for boys and girls through the age of 10, and "Junior" divisions for ages 11-16. Although not required for record submission, a low-cost junior membership program with its own bimonthly newsletter was also initiated. By the year 2001, junior IGFA members populated more than 50 countries, enjoying their own contests, receiving their own mail, and visiting their own website.

[10]Including 50 freshwater and 50 saltwater; the numbers have since more than doubled. Junior records are all-tackle only and do not include line class consideration.

Recognizing the ongoing need for new anglers to perpetuate the sport, Leech crafted the IGFA's new junior program with care. Rather than focusing on a one-time experience, the program was and remains geared to creating a lifelong enthusiasm for recreational angling. A medley of various elements combined to teach ethical fishing practices at a young age, add to angling skills, and create an awareness of the importance of conservation.[11] As Leech knew it would, the initiative also served to soften the IGFA's image, increase family memberships, and stimulate financial largesse. Among the most visible early sponsors was well-known charter boat captain Tred Barta who dedicated proceeds from his Blue Marlin Classic Tournament to the IGFA's Junior Angler Program shortly after its inception in 1997. As Mike Leech had foreseen, educating and attracting young would-be anglers was not only good work but also good business.

---

[11] *Unlike adult world record requirements, juniors were encouraged to catch, weigh and release their record fish.*

IGFA President Mike Leech congratulates a pair of diminutive junior anglers.

IGFA wants YOU!

Now your company can proudly display its associ...
with the world's most respected fishing organiza...

IGFA Corporate Membe...

Companies can show their support for IGFA's many programs that bene...
ational fishermen by becoming Corporate Members. All Corporate ...
receive the right to use the IGFA Corporate Member logo to promote bu...
Certificate of Membership, discount on advertising in the *Internationa*...
newsletter, facility rental discount at the IGFA Fishing Hall of Fame & ...
and individual memberships and advertising ...
Fishes book determined by ...

Level 1 - $550 includes ...
Record Game Fishes, a ...
right to use the IGFA c...

Level 2 - $1,100 include...
Record Game Fishes, a ...
right to use the IGFA co...

Level 3 - $1,650 includes...
Game Fishes, a certifica...
the IGFA corporate men...

Level 4 - $2,200 includes...
Record Game Fishes, a ce...
to use the IGFA corporat...

Level 5 - $2,750 includes...
Game Fishes, seven indivi...
use the IGFA corporate m...

❑ Yes, I want to become...
IGFA programs dedicated ...

My check is enclosed for $_____
Please bill my credit card ❑ Visa ❑ ...

Account No. ┌─┬─┬─┬─┬─┬─┐

Name of Company:_____
Attention: (Executive's name and title)_
Street Address:_____
City/State:_____
Telephone:_____
Please enclose names of company offic...
_____
_____

IGFA • 300 Gulf Stream ...
(Phone) 954-92...
HQ@IGFA...

BECOME AN IGFA CERTIFIED CAPTAIN/GUIDE

International Ga...
Fishing Hall of ...
300 Gulf ...
Dania Beach, ...

INTERNATIONAL GAME FISH ASSOCIATION

OFFICIAL WEIGH STATION PROGRAM

WHERE THERE'S FISHING, THERE'S IGFA

INTERNATIONAL GAME FISH ASSOCIATION
FISHING HALL OF FAME & MUSEUM
300 Gulf Stream Way, Dania Beach, Florida 33004 USA
Phone (954) 927-2628 • Fax (954) 924-4299
E-mail: IGFAHQ@aol.com • Website: www.igfa.org

Among many other new programs initiated by Leech were those offering IGFA certification to boat captains and weigh stations.

As with all previous administrations, requests for changes to the angling rules continued during Leech's tenure, and even the most intemperate suggestions were duly considered. Most related to fly-fishing, as fly casters were constantly introducing new techniques gleaned from other areas of angling into their sport. Among other fly-fishing decisions Leech presided over were the banning of "dropper" flies, the exclusion of applied scents,[12] and the prohibition of flying gaffs. This latter ruling generated much controversy as such gaffs had originally been permitted but were subsequently disallowed when fly-fishing greats Stu Apte, Lefty Kreh, Billy Pate, Mark Sosin, and others arose in protest. "Fly fishing does not mean unlimited tackle," noted Sosin in an interview, and he bemoaned the efforts of some to use fly tackle in the pursuit of blue water giants. Leech and the IGFA agreed, maintaining the maximum tippet class for world record consideration at a relatively light 10kg (20-lb) ever since.

As the decade drew to a close, the IGFA paused in the late 1990s to take stock of its internal philosophies. While the organization remained dedicated to the principles of conservation, some within the IGFA felt that the presence of so many weight-related clubs (e.g., the Thousand Pound Club) was sending the wrong message. After considerable debate, IGFA Trustees voted in 1999 to eliminate several such clubs and subsequently discontinued the Annual Fishing Contest the following year. Shortly thereafter, the Certified Observer Program (COP) was conceived as a further nod to conservation and, in this at least, the decision was inspired. The COP was designed to encourage money tournaments to switch from capture to catch-and-release formats, previously unthinkable due to the enormous sums of money frequently at stake. Now a tournament offering substantial prize money could utilize independent and certified observers to ensure the competition's integrity without needlessly destroying dozens of game fish. Early reviews on the use of IGFA-certified observers were almost universally positive, and more and more tournaments began to utilize same. As the move towards catch-and-release continues to grow, the COP has the potential to develop into one of the IGFA's most important conservation initiatives.

IGFA
CERTIFIED OBSERVER PROGRAM

INTERNATIONAL GAME FISH ASSOCIATION
300 GULF STREAM WAY
DANIA BEACH, FLORIDA 33004, USA
PHONE: 954-927-2628 • FAX: 954-924-4299
E-MAIL: IGFAHQ@AOL.COM • WEBSITE: WWW.IGFA.ORG

167

---

[12]*Prohibited due to the reason that scents were not traditional to fly-fishing.*

Construction of the IGFA's new home on this ex-Superfund cleanup site took two years.

Despite this array of accomplishments, Mike Leech's most significant achievement was seeing to the completion of the IGFA Fishing Hall of Fame & Museum in Dania Beach, Florida. Leech's predecessor Elwood Harry was a compulsive collector of fishing artifacts and had long talked about establishing a permanent repository of angling history. At one point, IGFA Trustees had even authorized Harry to make limited expenditures towards developing such a facility, but he never found the time to do so. Upon Harry's death, Leech seized the initiative by asking a local architect to create preliminary plans for a sparkling landmark structure. With plans in hand, Leech attended his first Trustee meeting as IGFA's President and, by positioning the building as a fulfillment of Harry's original vision, gained their unanimous enthusiasm. The plan for an IGFA world headquarters was first unveiled to the public in 1993 with no specific location and an estimated cost of between $8-$10 million. The final result would be quite different.

After six years of fund-raising and two years of construction, the IGFA Fishing Hall of Fame & Museum opened in January of 1999. The 60,000 square foot structure was and remains truly breathtaking: a world-class facility in every way. Due largely to a team of wildly optimistic consultants, the building had been doubled in size from its earliest conception to now accommodate 500,000 visitors per year. Designed by the New Orleans architectural firm of Eskew Filson, its distinctive asymmetrical shape includes a soaring three-story roofline and polished stainless steel shingles done in a manner to suggest fish scales. Angular wooden slats in the lobby recall the planking of a boat's hull, and a shimmering finish to the walls and floor convey a sense of being within a massive aquarium. Outside, a 24' stainless steel swordfish designed by noted sculptor Kent Ullberg leaps skyward, an awe-inspiring sight and centerpiece of the entire complex. Ullberg's original sculpture was to be bronze but was later changed to high-grade stainless steel in deference to the strength of this ultimate sport fish. In doing so, he created the largest stainless steel game fish sculpture in the world.

Ullberg applies a final polish prior to installation.

169

IGFA President Mike Leech (left) with Kent Ullberg prior to Sword Dance *going vertical.*

The IGFA's magnificent Hall of Fame & Museum with
Kent Ullberg's signature sculpture in front.

The expansive grounds now surrounding Ullberg's swordfish are equally impressive. Formerly a lumber yard and toxic waste site, the conversion of this 14-acre facility into an ecological showcase was an enormous undertaking, but the result was (and is) nothing short of remarkable. Elements include a miniature marina and three acres of interconnected lakes, waterways, and wetlands that serve as habitat for dozens of species of flora and fauna. Among the local residents are five alligators, added in 2002 and evidently most comfortable in their new surroundings. However, their presence has thinned the duck population, originally begun with 15 ducklings ordered from a mail-order firm in Wisconsin and hand-raised by the Leeches for six weeks prior to release. More than a dozen species of voracious fish have also taken their toll, creating a miniature aquatic life cycle unique within the cosmopolitan setting of south Florida.

Inside the facility, one of the Museum's defining features is an 18-minute film on the tranquility and joy that comes from recreational angling. Elegantly photographed at various remote locations by the award-winning firm Donna Lawrence Productions, it is not about capturing fish but rather celebrates a spirit of catch-and-release throughout the film. If conservation is its subliminal message, the film also does a superb job in blending the beauty and harmony that can be found in various types of angling, and it has played to spellbound audiences since its premier showing.[13] Despite their initial trepidation, Leech and the IGFA Trustees were justifiably thrilled with the finished product, vindicating both their faith in the filmmaker and the enormous investment made in the film.

171

---

[13] *Interestingly, while the film features exceptional footage of a leaping "blue" marlin, the film crew was unable to capture enough suitable footage while on location. Thus, careful viewers will note that the blue marlin is actually a black marlin filmed in Australia.*

In addition to the theatre, the building's ground floor includes meeting rooms, a gift shop, and seven galleries filled with interactive displays of angling history, all leading into the Museum's spectacular Hall of Fame great-room. Leech had originally proposed the idea of a Hall of Fame to Harry but the latter vetoed it, worried that the politics of deciding upon inductees would be too much to bear. Nevertheless, the Hall of Fame became a cornerstone of the building's design, and its roster of 29 original inductees has grown to more than 55 since the facility opened in 1999. Above the Hall of Fame is the majestic Hall of Fishes,[14] a sweeping array of more than 170 mounted game fish looking down upon the proceedings below. Originally suggested by the architect and quickly endorsed by the Trustees, it fell to IGFA staffers to locate the many double-sided mounts that were required. Their worldwide search yielded countless stories.

Among other things, the staff soon learned to its dismay that the global supply of certain such mounts was extremely limited. Frustrated in his attempt to locate a suitably-mounted conger eel, Leech turned to the venerable British Conger Club for help and was ultimately rewarded with a proper specimen. Despite searching everywhere he could imagine, Leech was also thoroughly thwarted in his search for a mounted madai,[15] so he

---

[14]*The name was borrowed from an earlier display at the American Museum of Natural History sponsored by Lerner.*

[15]*A small species of bream generally found in waters off Japan.*

An upward view of the IGFA Museum Hall of Fishes.

Mike Leech compares dental work with the Museum's enormous great white shark.

arranged for a Japanese angler to catch a decent example and send it along to Australia for taxidermy before being shipped to Florida. The mounts of two enormous game fish — Alfred Dean's 2,664 lb white shark and Paulo Amorim's 1,402 lb blue marlin — were so large that they had to be inserted into the Hall of Fishes prior to the building's completion and closure. In fact, no mount even existed of Dean's giant shark, so a replica was created from an even larger 3,500 lb leviathan landed by legendary shark hunter Frank Mundus of *Jaws* fame. When Dean's widow attended the Museum's opening and saw what was ostensibly her husband's world record shark looming overhead, she sniffed and announced to her companion that, "Of course, my husband's fish was MUCH bigger than that."

174

Despite opening to much fanfare in January of 1999, attendance at the IGFA's Fishing Hall of Fame & Museum did not meet initial estimates and its $32 million price tag quickly proved to be burdensome. Nevertheless, that the building was completed at all is an enormous testament to the vision and generosity of the IGFA's Board of Trustees. The land was donated by IGFA Trustee John L. Morris, and the capital campaign to finance construction was led by Board Chairman George Matthews and then-IGFA Trustee Don Tyson, the latter setting an extraordinary personal example with his own largesse. Board member (and later Chairman) Mike Levitt was also crucial in his conception, promotion, and financing of the project. Many observers feel that the IGFA will grow into a multi-purpose facility over time, and indeed the building already serves well in housing the ever-expanding E. K. Harry Library of Fishes on its second floor and IGFA headquarters atop that. Despite its perhaps inevitable growing pains, the Museum remains a source of wonder and inspiration to all who visit it.

In many respects, Leech's tenure was a decade full of IGFA milestones. In 1994, Ann Kunkel was elected to the IGFA Board of Trustees, the first woman so recognized since Francesca LaMonte in 1974.[16] The following year, IGFA Trustee and veteran angler Stewart Campbell crushed Bill Carpenter's 32-year-old record by catching an astounding 73 giant bluefin

---

[16] *Ten years later, the IGFA Board would include three women members: Terri Andrews, Pam Basco, and Joan Wulff. Kunkel died in 1995.*

tuna in a single day. Fishing aboard *Raptor* with veteran charter boat captain Peter Wright, Campbell was hooked up almost continuously for more than 11 hours. All 73 fish were released. In May of 1999, Herbert G. Ratner Jr. became the first angler to set 100 IGFA world records, a remarkable accomplishment that fulfilled a 17-year quest. The next year, baseball great Ted Williams became the first living inductee to the IGFA Hall of Fame, with legendary living anglers Pierre Clostermann and Alfred C. Glassell Jr. following shortly thereafter.

With the building completed and his life's work largely in place, Leech stepped down as IGFA President in 2003 to assume the role of Ambassador-at-Large. A vast array of programs was begun during Leech's tenure, the results of which included a near doubling of worldwide membership. In addition to overseeing a massive construction project, he maintained a full Presidential workload, kept to a punishing travel schedule, and greatly increased the IGFA's significance in the environmental arena. Thus, in any number of areas did Mike Leech prove to be an able successor to the outstanding men who went before him. In his efforts to enhance membership value, protect the resource, and promote the pastime of recreational angling, the IGFA could hardly have asked for more.

Gussie and Mike Leech prepare to release another one.

WWW.IGFA.ORG   **WWW.IGFA.ORG**

THE IGFA RULE BOOK

For freshwater, saltwater, and fly fishing

INTERNATIONAL ANGLING RULES • WORLD RECORD
WORLD RECORD AND STATE FRESHWATER AP
GRAND SLAM CLUBS • 10 POUND BASS (
10 POUND BONEFISH CLUB • 25 POUND SNC

INTERNATIONAL GAME FISH ASS

Fishng Hall of Fame & Museum, 300 Gulf Stream Way, Dani
Phone 954-927-2628 Fax 954-924-4299 E-mail: HQ@igfa.

The current IGFA rule book along with an
out-of-print Spanish language translation
printed in the mid-1990s.

REGLAS INTERNACIONALES
DE LA IGFA
para la pesca en agua dulce y en el mar, y la pesca con mosca

REGLAS INTERNACIONALES DE PESCA • DISPOSICIONES VIGENTES PARA LOS
RECORDS DE PESCA • REGLAS PARA EL CONCURSO ANUAL DE PESCA IGFA
SOLICITUD DE REGISTRO DE RECORDS MUNDIALES Y DEL CONCURSO
CLUB DE MIL LIBRAS • CLUBS DE 5-1, 10-1, 15-1, 20-1 • CLUBS DE GRAN SLAM
CLUB DE LUBINA DE 10 LIBRAS • CLUB DE ROBALO DE 25 LIBRAS
PROGRAMA DE PESCADORES JUVENILES DEL RECORD MUNDIAL

INTERNATIONAL GAME FISH ASSOCIATION
(ASOCIACION INTERNACIONAL DE PESCA DEPORTIVA)

IGFA, 1301 East Atlantic Blvd., Pompano Beach, Florida 33060
Tel (954) 941-3474   Tolefax (954) 941-5868
E-Mail IGFA igfa.netcom.com

Chapter Nine

THE RULES OF ANGLING

The essential difference between angling and fishing can be captured in a single word: rules. According to the all-knowing *Oxford English Dictionary*, fishing as an activity is "the action, art, or practice of catching fish." Undeniably true, but when fishing is performed with rod and reel, it can become something altogether different: the contemplative art of angling. Add a framework of rules that promotes fair competition, and angling transcends contemplation to become a sport. Like baseball or bowling, angling with rod and reel can be purely recreational or, in keeping with human nature, elevated to a highly-competitive platform. When the latter occurs, angling as a sport requires all the rules and regulations of any other sport to maintain fairness. If all parties follow the same rules, then it becomes possible to assess individual accomplishments relative to one another, thus allowing for such benchmarks as competitions and world records. In short, an equitable set of rules brings organization and common ground to any activity and makes competitive sports out of some. In the case of angling, the existence and worldwide acceptance of IGFA rules have made it the great and popular sport that it is today.

Prior to 1939, however, there were no universally accepted rules of angling. Nevertheless, as Michael Lerner and the original IGFA organizers sat down to address the issue, they had a place to start. The Tuna Club of Catalina Island had already been in existence for more than 40 years; their angling rules were rigorously drawn and clearly well established.[1] Although not as venerable, the British Tunny Club was also underway and had its own ideas as to what constituted proper and sporting rules. From Mike Lerner's perspective, neither set was perfect. The IGFA's goal was to establish rules strict enough to define the sport but not so restrictive as to exclude new interest and participation. Indeed, it seemed clear that the simplest set of rules upon which all parties could agree would be the best. Thus, while Tuna Club rules served as the foundation, the IGFA softened their more restrictive aspects to create a broader all-inclusive framework for the sport as a whole. It was difficult work, and it took the IGFA almost four years to convert a wealth of ideas and opinions into final form.

Outdoor Life editor Tommy Aitken was recruited to pen the first draft, and he labored long and hard at the task. Aitken had been recognizing angling accomplishments and opportunities in his column for many years, and he had done much to publicize the early angling activities off Bimini and elsewhere. After much input by the IGFA's Executive Committee and others, Aitken's final version consisted of 11 rules and was published as gospel in the IGFA's inaugural yearbook in 1943. They were as follows:

1. *Acceptable line must be of the 50 lea linen variety and classified by thread count.*
2. *Double line cannot be longer than leader or trace.[2]*
3. *Rods must be constructed of wood or cane.*
4. *The angler must hook, fight and bring to gaff the fish without assistance.*
5. *Change to the rod or reel or the splicing of line during the fight is prohibited.*
6. *No more than two (2) single hooks may be used in any one bait, and these must be attached at least one (1) shank's length apart.*
7. *Use of a float is prohibited except those used in regulating the depth of a bait.*
8. *Resting of the rod on a boat's gunnel is prohibited.*
9. *Use of the boat engine to drag or lift a fish is prohibited.*

---

[1] *Tuna Club rules were thought to be penned by legendary angler Jimmy Jump in 1906.*
[2] *Soon changed to a 25' maximum limit for each and periodically revised thereafter.*

DESERT PRONGHORN — — — — — — — — BEN TINKER
CATALINA SWORDFISH — — — — — — — DR. J. A. WIBORN

An early issue of Outdoor Life *featuring an article on swordfishing off Catalina. IGFA rules author Tommy Aitken served as the magazine's Big Game Fishing Editor for many years.*

10. Use of a detachable ("flying") gaff is permitted if gaff length does not exceed 8' in length and does not include more than 30' of attached rope.

11. The following events will disqualify the catch from record consideration: (a) failure to comply with rules or tackle specifications as outlined above; (b) use of a broken rod or one broken during the fight; (c) anyone other than the angler touching or handling the angler's tackle (except the leader as the fish is being gaffed); (d) hand-lining a hooked fish by anyone at any time; (e) the shooting, harpooning or lancing of a hooked fish; (d) mutilation by shark.

Although most rules were consistent with the sporting practices of the day, a few were controversial. Many fishing captains and boatmen commonly subdued large fish by shooting them once they were alongside the boat, and the prohibition of this practice generated much debate. Large fish were dangerous, so the argument went, but good sportsmanship ultimately prevailed. Likewise, the use of flying gaffs was thought by some to convey an unfair advantage to the angler. Although designed to provide protection to the boatman, worry ensued that such gaffs could be hurled at hooked fish just out of normal gaffing range. While that concern proved to be

The I.G.F.A. Yearbook 1943

RULES OF THE INTERNATIONAL GAME FISH ASSOCIATION

WORLD RECORD CATCHES

In the past, world record catches have been based solely upon fish weight. In the future, a chart will be kept, giving credit and world recognition to each angler based on the tackle used, so that light tackle achievements shall receive the world recognition they merit.

It is proposed to classify catches on the basis of six different weights of line, as follows:

6-thread
9-thread
15-thread
24-thread
39-thread
54-thread

Recognition of record catches that may be made on line sizes between the approved standards will be entered on the next stronger weight *(for example:* catches made on 12-thread will qualify on 15-thread, etc.).

SHARKS, which are cartilaginous fishes, as opposed to other fishes which have bony skeletons, will be placed in a separate classification.

APPLICATIONS FOR WORLD RECORD

The location of officially qualified clubs or units will be available to all fishermen. Any application for a world record must be submitted to the Executive Committee and must be supported by statutory declarations from the angler, one witness, the boat captain, and the official weighmaster at the qualified unit or club for that section in which the fish is caught.

Such affidavit must state that the fish was caught by the person claiming the record, and strictly in accordance with the rules of the International Game Fish Association. Name of captor; date; place; weight, length and girth of fish; full particulars of tackle; clear photograph of the tackle, showing rod tip and butt, and photograph of the fish, must be included. In the case of a Shark, the photograph should show not only the full length of the fish, but its open mouth displaying the teeth.

108

Rules

In the event that it is impossible to bring a record fish before an accredited weighmaster for weighing, an affidavit sworn to by the angler and attested by two witnesses before a notary public, will receive full consideration by the Association. A photograph must in all cases accompany all entries. *No estimated weights will be accepted.*

In the event that a fish is caught from a yacht at sea, or under other extenuating conditions where it is impossible to bring the fish to a recognized weighing station, the affidavits of the captor, captain, mate and one witness will be accepted in lieu of the usual affidavit, providing that the affidavits include the fact that the scales used are attested scales.

In all other cases, the fish must be officially weighed on land by a recognized official of the section in which such weighing is being done. The actual tackle used must be exhibited to the local official weighmaster at the time of such weighing.

Any individual protest as to the method of weighing or manner in which a fish was caught must be made to the accredited local club or unit for survey.

Only fish caught in accordance with these rules shall be accepted as angling records. No catch will be accepted as an official World Record until the affidavit for it has been examined by at least two members of the Executive Committee.

Applications not complying with the above regulations and tackle specifications of the Association cannot be considered.

From July 1, 1941, on, record claims for fish caught in *North American waters* will not be accepted by the I.G.F.A. if the date of the catch is over *sixty days* before the date of receipt of the affidavit by the I.G.F.A. Claims for fish caught in *other waters* will not be accepted if the date of the catch is over *three months* before the date of receipt of the affidavit by the I.G.F.A. Delays due to war conditions will be given special consideration.

The International Game Fish Association cannot participate in the awarding of any trophies or prizes in which the name of any advertised product is directly or indirectly concerned.

NO OFFICER OR MEMBER OF THE EXECUTIVE COMMITTEE MAY HOLD ANY WORLD GAME FISH RECORD AS LONG AS HE SHALL BE AN OFFICER OR MEMBER OF THE EXECUTIVE COMMITTEE. (This rule does not apply to members of the International Committee).

109

Aitken's original angling rules as they appeared in the IGFA's first yearbook in 1943.

unwarranted, their inclusion as permissible tackle was allowed only after restrictions on length were added. All in all, however, the rules were simple, easy to understand and promoted a more equal contest between man and fish: just the result that the IGFA sought. Also as intended, any angler catching a large enough fish under such rules was eligible for world record recognition.[3]

Once Aitken's framework was in place, early modifications to the rules were largely decided by a vote of member clubs and International Representatives. When Fin-Nor introduced its innovative double-handled reel in the 1940s, the IGFA's Executive Committee felt that the new innovation extended an unfair advantage to the angler in leverage and torque. Subsequently, the membership was polled and found to be in overwhelming agreement with this opinion. As a result, the newfangled reels were promptly banned. On the other hand, a lack of timely action sometimes yielded unanticipated results. When Frank O'Brien of Tycoon Rods first introduced the now-standard bent butt rod design at the request of Bimini anglers, it was derided as freakish by IGFA elders who felt certain it would die a natural death. Nevertheless, despite its odd appearance, O'Brien's innovation did accomplish its purpose of adding leverage by reducing the functional rod length, and less-experienced big-game anglers took to it handily. By the time the IGFA revisited the matter, it had been universally embraced.

---

[3]Despite some calls to the contrary, the IGFA has never discriminated in granting world record holder status to professional boatmen so long as the catch was made in accordance with IGFA rules.

One of the more significant innovations to generate controversy was the introduction of fiberglass rods in the late 1940s. While IGFA rules offered little guidance at that time relative to rods except to require wood or cane construction, the Tuna Club of Catalina had maintained stringent requirements on the subject since the turn of the century. Worried that the powerful new fiberglass rods would provide anglers with an unfair advantage, the Tuna Club prohibited their use until long-time members Bill Pigg and George C. Thomas III came up with a plan. Through the use of a deflection board, the two anglers were able to compare the relative strengths of fiberglass and wood rods, even to the extent of demonstrating that certain fiberglass rods could be too strong for lighter line classes. When the two types of rods were thus compared, the Tuna Club and later the IGFA were able to create suitable standards for the new rods and allow for their use.

Less eventful was the invention of nylon and the subsequent introduction of monofilament and dacron fishing lines. Again following the Tuna Club's lead, the IGFA originally required that record submissions include the use of 50 lea[4] thread linen line. At the time, there was little alternative since silk line was the only other type of line widely available and was generally not suitable for saltwater use. The manufacturing process was also complicated, as linen line needed to be painstakingly woven in bundles of three individual threads, each of which had a breaking strength of approximately three pounds.[5] Nevertheless, the quality of linen line varied greatly from year to year, subject as it was to inconsistencies in manufacturing and vagaries in the annual flax crop from Ireland and Belgium. When actually put to use it was even more troublesome, offering virtually no stretch, breaking at greater stress levels when wet than dry, absorbing water at an alarming rate, and featuring the disconcerting tendency to rot unless thoroughly dried after exposure to moisture. As a result, the use of linen line was one of the most expensive and problematic elements of early big-game angling,[6] and almost all parties were delighted to adopt the new synthetic lines once consistency had been proven to everyone's satisfaction.

---

[4] *The unit of measure (by weight) for linen thread; a single 300 yard strand of 50 lea thread weighs less than 1/3 oz.*
[5] *Thus, "6-thread" linen had a breaking strength of approximately 18 lb.*
[6] *Today, the idiosyncratic Tuna Club stands alone as the last big-game angling organization to recognize and reward the use of linen line.*

Despite its odd appearance, the bent butt rod quickly became a favorite of heavy-tackle anglers.

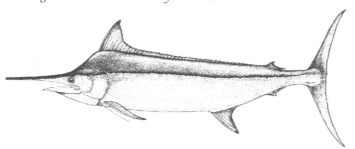

IMPORTANT NOTICE

THE INTERNATIONAL GAME FISH ASSOCIATION
Address: THE AMERICAN MUSEUM OF NATURAL HISTORY
79th Street and Central Park West
New York 24, N. Y., U. S. A.

RELEASE

July 29, 1948

RELEASED FOR immediate use (primarily submitted for your opinion).

You will find herewith a photograph of a new type of rod butt on which the International Game Fish Association earnestly solicits your judgment.

This butt, as you will see from the picture, is curved. It is used largely in taking tuna. It gives the angler a point of maximum lift at the most advantageous arc of the rod -- that is, when the tip is lower than is the case in the conventional rod-reel-harness combination. Fighting a big fish is made somewhat easier, as the user of a rod of this type does not have to lean back so far as he pumps.

The point on which we solicit your opinion is this: IS THIS INNOVATION ACCEPTABLE AS SPORTSMANLIKE TACKLE ?

It makes no change in line-strength factors -- or any other factors than angle of lift. The I.G.F.A. does not wish to be over-conservative or to stand in the way of modern and improved fishing tackle, and since the use of a curved butt is a departure from classical tackle, it is therefore of sufficient importance to be brought to the attention of a large jury.

The curved butt is being manufactured and used now in Florida by a reputable tackle concern, and if a fish of world record weight is taken on such tackle (conventional save for the curved butt) we shall be asked to decide whether or not the fish is eligible for such a record.

What would your judgment be ? Upon a larger concensus than our own opinions we intend to make the decision, in pursuance of our constant zeal in the maintenance of just and suitable angling rules.

We would greatly appreciate an early reply from you and from any other interested and competent parties to whom you might refer.

THE EXECUTIVE COMMITTEE I.G.F.A.

address replies to :..........................Francesca LaMonte, Secretary

By the time the IGFA circulated this questionnaire about bent butt rods in 1948, it was too late.

Still, there were dissenters. Many existing world record holders raised the point that improvements in tackle would make the capture of record-size fish too easy, taking away from their accomplishments on relatively inferior tackle. The Tuna Club was particularly incensed, arguing that the smaller diameter, smoother surface, and spring-like stretch of synthetic lines took all the skill out of angling. Nevertheless, after much debate on the subject, the IGFA finally concluded that it had a universal obligation to promote sportsmanlike standards as broadly as possible. While regrettable, the loss of world records to superior tackle (if not superior skill) was a cost worth bearing if the sport was to move forward, and the IGFA's acceptance of the new materials helped fuel the post-war surge in angling effort. If the former world record holders could find small consolation anywhere, it may have been in the fact that not all innovations worked very well at first. Early fiberglass rods had a disconcerting tendency to fracture or even snap while in use, and the binding nature of nylon line under stress would often crack its underlying spool and paralyze the reel.

The Tycoon rod factory was state-of-the-art in its manufacture of premium quality bamboo rods.

Frank O'Brien, President of Tycoon Tackle Inc. in Miami, admires a sampling of his factory's bamboo handiwork.

Despite the IGFA's ostensibly democratic structure when it came to rules, rank still had its privileges. As a committed heavy-tackle angler, Mike Lerner was not naturally disposed towards rules that favored light-tackle devotees. Thus, when a proposal was received from light-tackle interests that a single individual should serve as both wireman and gaffer (as per Tuna Club rules), Lerner objected on the grounds that the nature of big fish and heavy tackle made this a two-person job. Not surprisingly, his views on the matter prevailed, and IGFA rules today still favor big fish in allowing for more than one gaffer in addition to a wireman. Nevertheless, democracy had its way in 1961 when a rule limiting the maximum breaking strength of leader was first approved by a small handful of member clubs but later rescinded in a worldwide howl of protest.

That same year (1961) also saw the rescinding of a curious rule that attempted to match reel size to a given line class. The idea was to restrict the use of oversized and thus inappropriate reels in the capture of small and medium-sized fish. However, such a ruling was hardly necessary given that large reels at that time were very heavy and experienced anglers used them only when required. While that rule was quickly repealed, it was followed a few years later by the introduction of the idea of "balanced tackle." First appearing as a "suggestion" and by 1967 as a requirement, balanced tackle provided specifications in reel size, line strength, and leader strength for five tackle categories: extra-light, light, medium, heavy and extra-heavy. While not a bad idea in concept, it proved cumbersome in application and was eventually abandoned in favor of the more generic requirement that rods and reels comply with generally-accepted sporting customs and ethics. Thus do angling rules ebb and flow.

Nonetheless, from its first publication in 1943 until the assimilation of freshwater and fly records in 1978, the IGFA's fundamental rules of angling changed remarkably little. Most of the new regulations had to do with specific innovations in tackle: nylon lines (permitted), composite rods (ditto), power-driven reels (banned), audio-enhanced lures (allowed), and entangling devices (forbidden). Changes to the basic rules largely were in response to unsportsmanlike techniques: thus, practices such as herding a hooked fish into shallow water, intentionally foul-hooking a fish, and "fighting" a fish such that the double line never leaves the rod tip were outlawed. Still, other than those modifications needed to address developments in tackle or technique, the rules of angling at the dawn of 1978 were much like those of 35 years before.

185

Ashaway's famous "line walk", a 725' building adjacent to the main factory where its world-famous linen line was handwoven from individual threads.

Rushford, N.Y., July 20, 1946.

Dear Erl:

Etil To keep your records straight and also to give the guy
who holds the 1946 Bimini marlin record his due, these words:

You reported (via Neville Stuart) that Bill Lewis of NYC
had caught a ~~xxxx~~ 600-lb marlin recently in Bimini.

Bill's fish was mutillated. Bill's a friend of mine and
would want the facts published. He fished in Bimini for ten days
or so without a strike - and was justly pleased to hook and fight
a big blue. When he came in that evening - he celebrated his near-
success. He flew north early the next morning and his fish was
chopped up for bill and tail mounts and for bait before I got a
chance to measure it.

He fought the blue on or near the surface for about an
hour and a half. He was unable to bring it to boat in that time.
It finally sounded. At a depth of about 1,200 feet, sharks took
off a foot-wide circle of meat around the tail, leaving only skeleton,
a hunk of the shoulder, and opened up the gut. Thus the marlin *must*
~~must~~ have bled to death on bottom ~~in minutes~~ Bill horsed it up
and brought it in. It weighed, in that condition, 385-lbs. Estimates
of its actual weight ran around five hundred and up to six. *(marlin)*

It should also be said, I think, that, during the scrap,
Bill was assisted by the mate, who operated the star drag and led
the line by hand onto the reel. Bill is new to ~~florida~~ fishing and
I am positive that he did not know this sort of assistance from
the mate would have disqualified his fish.

At the International Game Fish Association we often have
to reject world record applications owing to the fact that the angler
has innocently had some such illegal aid from skippers and mates
who know better or ~~xxxixinly~~ should know better than to give it.
Certainly it is not asking too much to require that from the moment
of the strike, the angler handle his own rod, reel and line unassisted,
until the fish is brought to net or gaff, whether it be a brook
trout or a big marlin.

In this connection, I was surprised myself to find not
long ago that two reputable Miami boatmen had let out for me a bonefish
bait on a double line of 39-thread measuring about a hundred feet.
While I know post-war line is still unreliable, I would have had to
claim any catch on that rig as a 78-thread take. Luckily, I didn't
get a hit. ~~XXXX~~ A one-month look around this summer reveals that quite
a few boatmen seem to be letting down on the rules, on sportsmanship,
and trying for fish in any fashion and at all costs. Facts on fish
unfairly caught always leak eventually, such fish are scratched off,
and the ~~xxxxixni~~ result is embarrassment.

It was good to talk to you the other day. So many people
arrived that we got no chance to call Maybelle. But we'll see you
both in not too many weeks. All the best -- as ever ---

Phil

July 25, 1946.

Mr. Philip Wylie,
Rushford, N. Y.

Dear Phil:

It was mighty kind of you to take the interest in
the Bill Lewis catch at Bimini, as expressed in your letter of
July 20. I am enclosing herewith my column that resulted from
it. You're dead right about the carelessness of reporting the
results of angling. I've been misled so many times by anglers,
guides and others, that I am getting pretty cynical about the
whole thing.

As I have sometimes pointed out in my column, the
sport of angling suffers from a lack of rules. Manufacturers
of angling gear could help the situation by standardizing on
certain specifications for rods, reels, lines, et cetera. But
they do not do so because they face a certain waste in production
under such standardization.

Take, for instance, golf, baseball or football:
These games are played with standard equipment and under strict
rules. Of course, these games have national associations that
prescribe the gear to be used and the rules under which the games
shall be played. The manufacturers make the gear according to
the prescriptions and the followers of the games play according
to the rules.

A golf pro would not for a moment think of teaching
a pupil sly tricks or ways to beat the rules. In a game, the

would not accept help from the pro, nor would any pro offer
help. But the same player will accept help from a fishing
and nearly every fishing guide will offer to help. It is
situation.

Several well-known fishing clubs have endeavored to
rules for angling and name specifications for standard rods,
and lines. However, while the members of such clubs have
under those rules and used the recommended equipment, the
number of anglers not members of the clubs do not even know
existence of the rules. The International Game Fish As-
tion has sponsored certain rules of ethics in angling and
to be used, but the average angler or guide knows nothing
them.

What the association needs is a crusader who can obtain
news publicity on rules and ethics, drumming them into the
public year after year until every angler and every fishing
will be advised and will do the right thing because they have
sold on the idea that it is the proper thing to do. That
cost some money, but the right kind of crusader could raise
necessary funds. Only in that manner will the average angler
aware of the association and its rules and ethics.

Well, I've sounded off at great length, Phil, but I
I'd "get it off my chest" ---as you do each Sunday. Regards
best wishes to Ricky and yourself. Let me hear from you if
you find time to write.

Erl Roman

---

*IGFA First Vice President Philip Wylie was a stickler for rules and conducted an extensive correspondence regarding same.
This exchange of letters between Wylie and Erl Roman is dated 1946 and corrects details of a catch that appeared in one of
Roman's columns.*

Much changed that year. Coinciding with the 1978 take-over of freshwater and other records, IGFA President Elwood Harry was anxious to reconcile the rules of angling for all different categories. The following year, he undertook a major canvassing of anglers around the world for input on both fresh and saltwater angling rules. The IGFA received hundreds of responses: some articulate and well-reasoned, others brief and pointed. All were ultimately reviewed with care, and many were instrumental in the IGFA's first major rules revision since its founding. Among the matters resolved based on angler feedback was the IGFA's decision not to maintain separate spinfishing records; those were later absorbed into the general freshwater category. Additionally, the permissible use of line backing was defined for the first time, and fly-fishing rules were expanded to encompass both fresh and saltwater settings. If nothing else, the IGFA's willingness to solicit anglers as to their views and listen to what they had to say served to reinforce its already rock-solid position as the supreme arbiter of angling decorum.

Harry's survey had some unanticipated consequences as well. For example, it became apparent from respondents in the Pacific Northwest that little attention had been paid to that region in the past. No local game fish had ever been accredited with record status by the IGFA until 1978 when the Pacific halibut was added to the rolls. The anadromous[7] nature of salmon had always made them difficult to classify, so no records existed in either the fresh or saltwater categories for chinook, coho, pink and chum salmon.[8] There were also none for rockfish, surf perch, Pacific cod, and starry flounder, all very popular sport fish for Pacific Northwest anglers. When these omissions were brought to Harry's attention by J.J. Ames,[9] the IGFA promptly responded and record categories for most major species were soon established.

187

---

[7] *Fish found in both fresh and salt water such as the sturgeon.*
[8] *The lack of world record status for a fifth species of salmon - the sockeye — was somehow thought less outrageous by respondents due to the fish's near-exclusive existence in fresh water.*
[9] *Fisheries biologist and then-President of the Olympia Game Fishing Club.*

One of the IGFA's new responsibilities that didn't require much immediate attention was the area of saltwater fly fishing. A formalized set of saltwater fly rules was already in existence, having been written by Mark Sosin and unveiled at the 1966 inaugural meeting of the Salt Water Fly Rodders of America. Working from a sketchy set of guidelines developed by the Rod and Reel Club of Miami, Sosin took suggestions from all sides and was ultimately able to put a thoughtful and balanced set of saltwater fly rules to paper. The weather was horrible at the Salty Fly Rodders convention, but that didn't stop all the world's great saltwater fly anglers from attending, including Stu Apte, Joe Brooks, Lefty Kreh, A.J. McClane, Sosin, Charles Waterman, Lee Wulff, and others. That Sosin's original rules survived this august group with little change until absorbed by the IGFA 12 years later[10] was no small feat. During the interim, Sosin also kept the association's saltwater fly records, conducting line tests as necessary and generally maintaining an admirable rigor in the administration of his own rules.[11]

---

[10] _And indeed until today._

[11] _Interestingly, no freshwater fly world records had ever been kept until the IGFA initiated same in 1981._

Today, input regarding proposed rule changes is solicited from all interested parties. So sacrosanct is the process that occasionally such surveys extend for months. Once comment has been gathered, the matter is discussed by the IGFA Rules Committee and referred to the entire Board of Trustees for a final decision. Occasionally, a universal standard is suggested for some element of tackle or cockpit equipment (e.g., standardizing the length of tagging sticks), but "guidelines" are issued instead of rules if there is no unanimity. In fact, tag sticks are a good example: one school of thought holds that longer tag sticks impart less stress to large fish, but others argue that tag sticks should be no longer than the maximum allowable length of a gaff (8'). After extensive research, the IGFA finally allowed regional preferences to apply, and tag sticks today can be found anywhere from 5' to 15' and even longer.

Since its inception, the IGFA has prided itself on no matter being too arcane to explore. In 1981, Elwood Harry and the IGFA Executive Committee considered at length whether salt or freshwater rules applied to the capture of anadromous fish,[12] extending tippet lengths for large saltwater fish caught on a fly (not approved due to the unfair advantage that would be gained by new record-seekers), and the prohibition of fly rods less than 6' in length (upheld). As an example of the IGFA's thoroughness in researching such matters, this last question was put to a number of experts for comment, and lengthy responses were received by such angling luminaries as Lefty Kreh, Mark Sosin, and A.J. McClane.

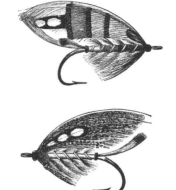

---

[12]*Freshwater rules were found to apply.*

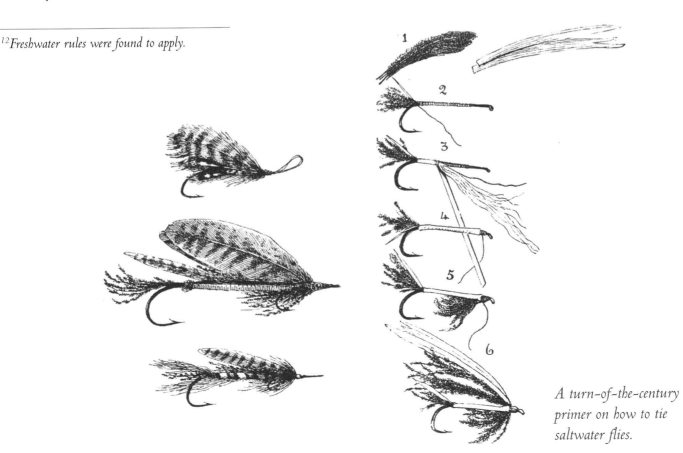

A turn-of-the-century primer on how to tie saltwater flies.

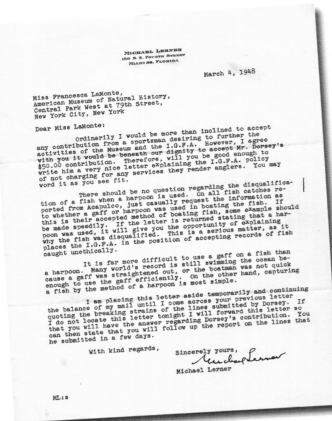

IGFA correspondence files are full of early letters from Mike Lerner to Francesca LaMonte regarding rules violations. This one takes issue with a 1948 record application where the fish had clearly been harpooned into submission.

Having withstood the test of time in admirable fashion, the IGFA's rules of angling have been reassuringly slow to change.[13] Nevertheless, new and heretofore unconsidered elements have surfaced over the years that have prompted periodic rule amendments. In 1981, the IGFA became aware that certain Florida boat captains had developed the practice of backing down full speed on larger fish hooked on light tackle. When coupled with the use of a lengthy double line and leader, this technique would often result in the fish being gaffed before any single line ever left the reel. Only slightly less egregious was the practice among western Pacific fishermen to cleat off a large fish once it was alongside the boat. Held fast by a lengthy leader, the fish would exhaust itself by towing the boat, thus allowing for a rapid capture with little effort expended by the angler. Harry had hoped to retire the use of double lines altogether to allow more of the fight to proceed on a single line. Nevertheless, amending the rules to limit the length of allowable double line and leader was more than enough to eliminate these and other unsportsmanlike practices.

190

---

[13] *And rarely in favor of the angler.*

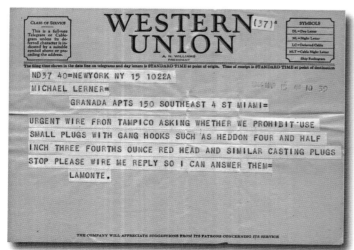
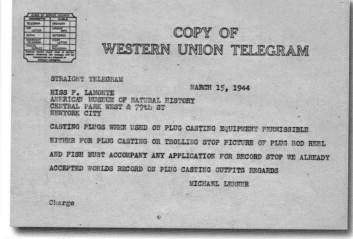

As evidenced by this exchange of telegrams between Francesca LaMonte and Mike Lerner, questions arose regarding spinfishing as early as 1944.

REPRINTED FROM OCTOBER, 1960, ISSUE OF **SPORTS AFIELD MAGAZINE**

SPOILSPORTS OF BIG-GAME FISHING

BY PHILIP WYLIE

THE GREAT AND FAST-GROWING sport of big-game fishing is being increasingly threatened by a special brand of chiseler. The rules for this sport are detailed, internationally agreed on, and available to anybody. So are the application forms by which the skillful (and perhaps, also, lucky) fishermen may enter their super-catches for a world record. But the record-robber doesn't quite understand, or quite accept, the spirit and intent of those international rules. The would-be tackle-crook reads the rules and notes the world-record application blank requirements. Then, he gets down to details. By ignoring a few printed principles of sportsmanship and by sticking to the exact letter of the detailed rules he realizes that he can go after some nearby species of fish or shark or sawfish (all listed as "game" for marine Waltonians) with very light tackle. He notes, after a study of "world-record catches" listed in many different categories of line strength, that he can perhaps snitch a "world record" for himself!

Applications, duly filled out and accompanied by the required photographs of the catch and a sample (for professional testing) of the line used—applications for records properly signed, attested, sworn to and notarized—reach the record-keeping organization, the International Game Fish Association, in ever-increasing number. But the catches for which such filled-in blanks claim records are also increasingly and very obviously not made by men who fished in a truly sportsmanlike manner, but by men who stooped to cheating, trickery and un-sporting methods.

The International Game Fish Association is distressed at this rise of chiseling in the sport it serves. I know. I happen to be one of the three Governors of the IGFA and a member of its Executive Committee. In order to understand the details of the chiselers' methods, one must first know something about the IGFA.

What I am about to confide I set down as an individual, not as an official. No member of any of

In addition to being a stickler for rules, Wylie was also passionate about angling ethics. This lengthy article espousing his views ran in a 1960 issue of Sports Afield *magazine.*

191

Occasionally, new techniques would emerge from obscurity to come under IGFA review. Although IGFA rules have always been clear in prohibiting anyone from assisting the angler, the rules were silent when it came to aiding the offshore angler in traversing a boat. A minor modification to the rule brought new clarity: while the angler must fight the fish unaided, assistance in circumnavigating the vessel was allowable. Likewise, bridge fishermen along southern Florida had developed the unusual technique of connecting their tackle to a buoy and casting the entire arrangement into the water if their hooked fish chose to run underneath the bridge. As the rig drifted below, the miscreant would run across the bridge, snag the buoy as it drifted by, and resume the fight. While this did not exactly constitute second-party aid to the angler, it did result in a new rule specifying that the catch would be judged in accordance with the heaviest of any two attached lines.

Still other modifications to the rules had their own unique origins. Double hooks were originally banned to eliminate the snagging of coho salmon and other tight-schooling species. Using any part of a mammal[14] as bait or chum was disallowed when it was discovered that some anglers were slaughtering seals, porpoises, cattle and other land animals to use as bait. The issue of whether or not a fish weighed at sea can be submitted for record consideration was decided in the negative for two reasons: first, because scale fluctuations due to hull stability were impossible to determine, and second, because such a practice if legal might encourage the wasteful discarding of fish at sea. Whatever the reasoning, the IGFA's overriding intent in any question of rules has always been to favor the fish instead of the angler, ever tightening the requirements so as to offset the advantages in tackle and technique that have accrued to anglers over the years.

---

[14]Except horse hair, pork rind and a very few other exceptions.

Early captures of huge sharks like this one taken off Australia in 20 minutes likely were the result of techniques no longer allowed today.

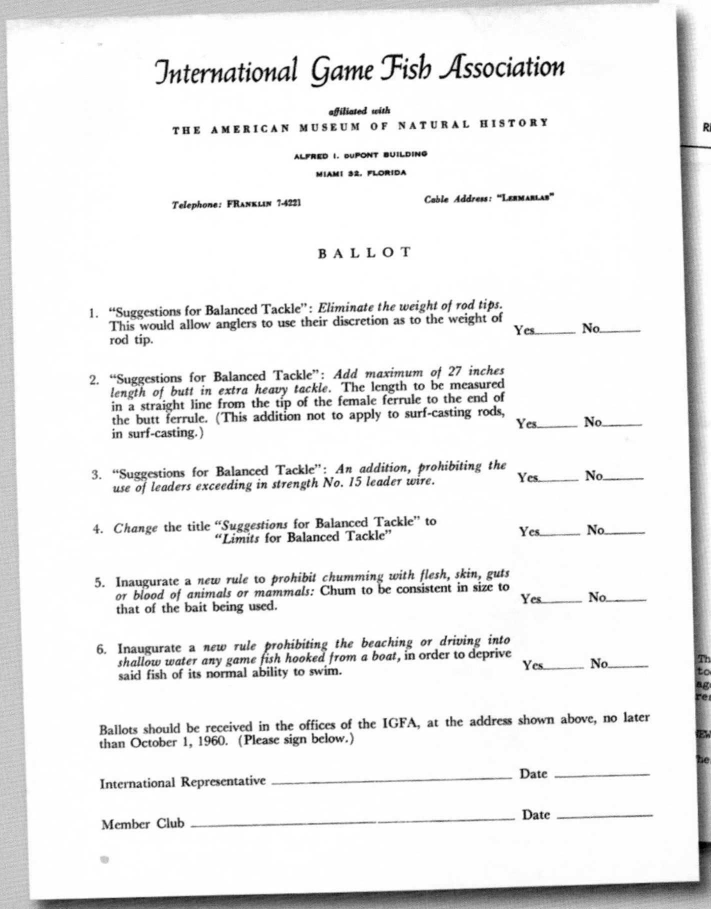

International Game Fish Association

affiliated with

THE AMERICAN MUSEUM OF NATURAL HISTORY

ALFRED I. DuPONT BUILDING

MIAMI 32, FLORIDA

Telephone: FRanklin 7-4221   Cable Address: "Lermarlas"

BALLOT

1. "Suggestions for Balanced Tackle": *Eliminate the weight of rod tips.* This would allow anglers to use their discretion as to the weight of rod tip.   Yes_____ No_____

2. "Suggestions for Balanced Tackle": *Add maximum of 27 inches length of butt in extra heavy tackle. The length to be measured in a straight line from the tip of the female ferrule to the end of the butt ferrule.* (This addition not to apply to surf-casting rods, in surf-casting.)   Yes_____ No_____

3. "Suggestions for Balanced Tackle": *An addition, prohibiting the use of leaders exceeding in strength No. 15 leader wire.*   Yes_____ No_____

4. *Change the title* "Suggestions for Balanced Tackle" *to* "Limits for Balanced Tackle"   Yes_____ No_____

5. Inaugurate a *new rule to prohibit chumming with flesh, skin, guts or blood of animals or mammals:* Chum to be consistent in size to that of the bait being used.   Yes_____ No_____

6. Inaugurate a *new rule prohibiting the beaching or driving into shallow water any game fish hooked from a boat,* in order to deprive said fish of its normal ability to swim.   Yes_____ No_____

Ballots should be received in the offices of the IGFA, at the address shown above, no later than October 1, 1960. (Please sign below.)

International Representative _____ Date _____

Member Club _____ Date _____

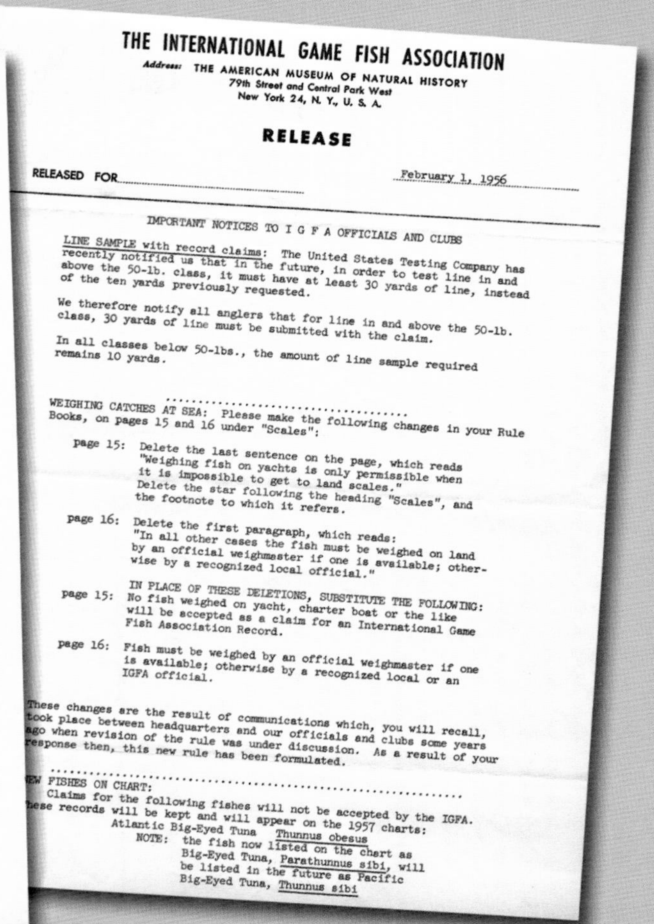

THE INTERNATIONAL GAME FISH ASSOCIATION

Address: THE AMERICAN MUSEUM OF NATURAL HISTORY
79th Street and Central Park West
New York 24, N. Y., U. S. A.

RELEASE

RELEASED FOR _____   February 1, 1956

IMPORTANT NOTICES TO I G F A OFFICIALS AND CLUBS

LINE SAMPLE with record claims: The United States Testing Company has recently notified us that in the future, in order to test line in and above the 50-lb. class, it must have at least 30 yards of line, instead of the ten yards previously requested.

We therefore notify all anglers that for line in and above the 50-lb. class, 30 yards of line must be submitted with the claim.

In all classes below 50-lbs., the amount of line sample required remains 10 yards.

WEIGHING CATCHES AT SEA: Please make the following changes in your Rule Books, on pages 15 and 16 under "Scales":

page 15: Delete the last sentence on the page, which reads "Weighing fish on yachts is only permissible when it is impossible to get to land scales." Delete the star following the heading "Scales", and the footnote to which it refers.

page 16: Delete the first paragraph, which reads: "In all other cases the fish must be weighed on land by an official weighmaster if one is available; otherwise by a recognized local official."

IN PLACE OF THESE DELETIONS, SUBSTITUTE THE FOLLOWING:

page 15: No fish weighed on yacht, charter boat or the like will be accepted as a claim for an International Game Fish Association Record.

page 16: Fish must be weighed by an official weighmaster if one is available; otherwise by a recognized local or an IGFA official.

These changes are the result of communications which, you will recall, took place between headquarters and our officials and clubs some years ago when revision of the rule was under discussion. As a result of your response then, this new rule has been formulated.

NEW FISHES ON CHART: Claims for the following fishes will not be accepted by the IGFA. These records will be kept and will appear on the 1957 charts. Atlantic Big-Eyed Tuna   Thunnus obesus NOTE: the fish now listed on the chart as Big-Eyed Tuna, Parathunnus sibi, will be listed in the future as Pacific Big-Eyed Tuna, Thunnus sibi

Prior to becoming a membership–based organization, the IGFA would poll its affiliated clubs and International Representatives as to proposed rule changes. While the process was not exactly democratic, the IGFA Tackle Committee would assign considerable weight to the results.

Indeed, such advances have not been trivial. Today's anglers fish from sleek boats with almost unimaginable arrays of electronic and fish-finding equipment. Reels have evolved from the primitive "knuckle-busters" used by early Tuna Club pioneers to multi-geared marvels of engineering. Rod materials have advanced even further, from cane poles to laminated bamboo to fiberglass to today's graphite and composite blends. Early fishing lines made from natural fibers such as cotton, hair, flax, gut, and silk compare most unfavorably with today's ultra-uniform and non-rotting braided hybrids. Even rod guides have been transformed from simple agate-lined rings to complex roller assemblies made from the most sophisticated alloys. The IGFA has worked diligently to review all such developments and generally has not hesitated to ban those that upset the sporting balance between angler and quarry.

Illustrated Guide to Equipment Regulations
DOUBLE LINES AND LEADERS

Double lines are measured from the start of the knot, braid, roll or splice making the double line to the farthermost end of the knot, splice, snap, swivel or other device used for securing the trace, leader lure or hook to the double line. A double line must consist of the actual line used to catch the fish. For saltwater species, the double line shall be limited to 15 feet (4.57 meters) for all line classes up to and including 20 lb (10 kg); and shall be limited to 30 feet (9.14 meters) for line classes over 20 lb (10 kg). For freshwater species, the double line on all classes of tackle shall not exceed 6 feet (1.82 meters).

The leader shall be limited to 15 feet (4.57 meters) for saltwater species in line classes up to and including 20 lb (10 kg), and 30 feet (9.14 meters) for all line classes over 20 lb (10 kg). For freshwater species, the leader on all classes of tackle shall be limited to 6 feet (1.82 meters).

The length of the leader is the overall length including any lure, hook arrangements or other device.

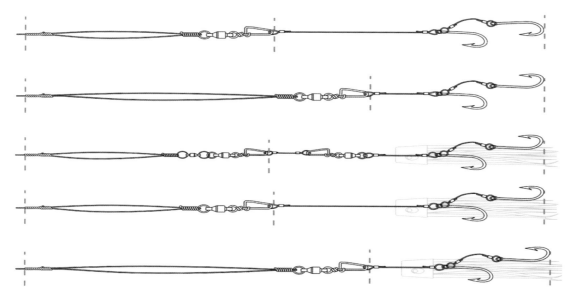

The combined length of the double line and leader shall not exceed 20 ft (6.1 meters) in line classes up to and including 20 lb (10 kg) and 40 feet (12.19 meters) in line classes over 20 lb (10 kg) for saltwater species. The combined length of the double line and leader shall not exceed 10 feet (3.04 meters) for freshwater species.

To clarify its rules on terminal tackle, the IGFA began to include illustrations on key rules in its 1986 World Record Game Fishes *publication.*

HOOKS

LEGAL if eyes of hooks no more than 18 inches (45.72 cm) apart in baits and no more than 12 inches (30.45 cm) apart in lures. ILLEGAL if eyes further apart than these distances.

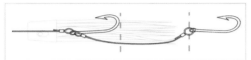

NOT LEGAL as the second or trailing hook extends more than the hook's length beyond skirt. See also two hook rigs.

NOT LEGAL in bait or lures as eyes of hooks are less than a hook's length (the length of the largest hook) apart.

LEGAL as eyes of hooks are no less than a hook's length apart and no more than 18 inches (45.72 cm) in baits and 12 inches (30.45 cm) in lures.

LEGAL in baits and lures. The point of one hook is passed through the eye of the other hook.

LEGAL as eyes of hooks are no less than a hook's length apart and no more than 12 inches (30.45 cm) apart, and the trailing hook does not extend more than a hook's length beyond the skirt.

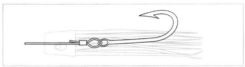

LEGAL as hook is contained within the skirt.

NOT LEGAL as the single hook extends more than its length beyond the skirt.

NOT LEGAL as back hook is not firmly imbedded in or securely attached to bait and is a dangling or swinging hook.

LEGAL as both hooks are firmly imbedded or securely attached to bait. Would not be legal if eyes of hooks were more than 18 inches (45.72 cm) apart.

GAFFS

LEGAL on boats if effective rope length does not exceed 30 feet (9.15 meters).

LEGAL on boats if overall gaff length does not exceed 8 feet (2.44 meters).

Many saltwater fly anglers view the tarpon as the largest quarry suitable for such tackle. Nevertheless, truly massive tarpon with scales the size of this one from Guinea-Bissau are exceedingly difficult to land on fly gear.

Today the rule book for such a varied and expansive sport as recreational angling remains remarkably brief. Barely two thousand words regulate the traditional sport with perhaps a thousand more needed to cover fly fishing. Changes in the modern era have been relatively few, and many of those have had to do with fly fishing for traditional big-game species. As this hybrid sport has increased in popularity, the IGFA has responded to certain practices that it has deemed unsportsmanlike. Examples of action taken in this regard include the 1998 ruling that prohibits the stripping of more than 120' of line from a fly reel after casting. This rule was in response to the practice of dropping a fly back to a sailfish following well beyond the angler's casting ability. Previously, flying gaffs approved for saltwater fly use were subsequently banned after reports of abuse, and other big-game-specific accessories such as shoulder harnesses have been discussed but never permitted in saltwater fly fishing. Indeed, such experts as Mark Sosin have periodically called into question the marriage of big-game fishing and fly tackle, arguing that angling with a fly was never meant to be a heavy-tackle sport. Nevertheless, that all of recreational angling with its countless variations can be governed by a small handful of rules says much for the IGFA's original approach.

As the sport of angling moves into the 21st century, new questions of rules continue to arise. Many larger game fishing boats now include a mechanically-propelled swivel device to aid in the movement of fighting chairs, but some fear this new development will lessen the importance of an attentive crew and add to an already dangerous cockpit environment. As these words are being written, the IGFA is once again gathering data and polling its members to understand their views on the matter.[15] Notwithstanding the fact that the organization is no longer privately funded (and thus more susceptible to outside pressure), the IGFA continues to make every effort to keep sportsmanship at the forefront of this and other as-yet unmade decisions. Whatever the ultimate ruling, there is little doubt that the IGFA's word will remain law and virtually all of the world's major sportfishing tournaments will continue to abide by its rules.

In the end, and despite the IGFA's deserving status as the governing body of recreational angling, the organization rightly recognizes that rules and records should not solely determine the quality of a given angling experience. In a long-appearing preface to its own angling rules written by the renowned Australian author and sportsman Peter Goadby, the IGFA delivers an eloquent reminder that angling should provide, above all, a most personal kind of satisfaction.

> *There are some aspects of angling that cannot be controlled through rule-making. Angling regulations cannot insure an outstanding performance from each fish, and world records cannot indicate the amount of difficulty in catching the fish. Captures in which the fish has not fought or has not had a chance to fight do not reflect credit on the fisherman, and only the angler can properly evaluate the degree of achievement in establishing the record.*

---

[15] *In its preliminary ruling, the IGFA's Rules Committee has decreed that the device does not provide material aid to the angler and is thus legal.*

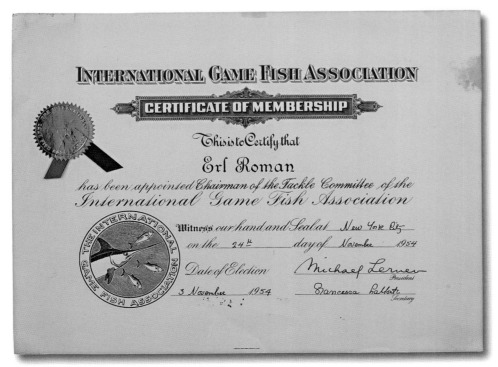

An appointment to the Tackle Committee is a most weighty assignment for IGFA Trustees. A symbol of its enduring importance is this 1954 certificate appointing Erl Roman as Tackle Committee Chairman.

Almost surely the IGFA's most famous all-tackle record, this 1,560 lb black marlin was taken by Alfred C. Glassell, Jr. in 1953.

Chapter Ten

THE STUFF OF RECORDS

All true sports have records, and recreational angling is no different. As evidenced by the enduring popularity of the *Guinness World Records*, there is great public affinity for such benchmarks and, in the case of sport fishing, much scientific value as well. Over the 60-plus years that IGFA records have been systematically kept, a great mass of data has been accumulated on the size, distribution, and growth of many game fish. Such information allows different fishing locales to be judged relative to one another and even serves to measure the health of a given fishery over time. Undoubtedly, the process of record-keeping has also affected decisions relative to conservation and forced anglers to become more knowledgeable in their identification of different species. Exceptional efforts have been recognized, heroes have been created, and considerable prestige has been conveyed with the granting of world record status. For some, the setting of an IGFA world record is the fulfillment of a lifelong quest.

While many gamefish species are easily identified, most anglers give little thought to the ichthyology behind some world record claims. Indeed, the identification of aquatic species is much more dynamic than most people know. As of October 2004, marine science had identified some 28,725 different finfish in the world,[1] including 4,321 of commercial importance, 202 unfortunate varieties commonly used as baitfish, and 1,134 species of sport fish. Every 10 years, the American Fisheries Society issues an exhaustive review of fish classifications, and changes are made all the time. Scientific names are often restated, and occasionally whole families are reclassified based on new analysis or research. Despite being first described in 1758, the broadbill swordfish has been reclassified at least eight times and still goes by hundreds of different local and regional names. More recently, political correctness has come into play with the renaming of squawfish (to pike-killing minnow) and jewfish (to goliath grouper). Sometimes name changes are made to reduce confusion, but the results are not always assured. The Australian snapper[2] was recently rechristened squirefish, much to the irritation of locals who were used to calling only juvenile snapper by that name.

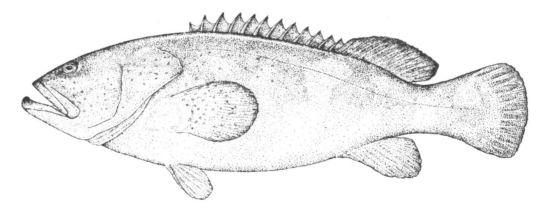

The renamed goliath grouper.

Also unknown to most anglers is that many species are still being discovered in places like the Amazon and through deep-water exploration. Advances in science have allowed ichthyologists to make finer and finer distinctions between species, sometimes down to the genetic level. Nevertheless, if a species is not commercially important, remarkably little about its life is often known. Anglers wax ecstatically about the fighting qualities of the tarpon, and the species has been a favorite of sport fishermen for more than 100 years. However, it became clear after a recent IGFA tarpon/bonefish symposium that almost nothing is known about the tarpon's habits. Virtually no information on its breeding and migratory patterns has ever been recorded, its spawning grounds are largely unknown, and no fertilized tarpon egg has ever been recovered.

---

[1] *Divided between 12,217 freshwater, 13,708 saltwater, and 2,800 diadromous or brackish-water species.*
[2] *Actually not a snapper at all but a member of the porgy family.*

The problem of species identification becomes even more distinct after reviewing the IGFA's 2004 list of 935 species for which all-tackle records are kept. The assortment includes 24 different species of catfish, 28 species of bass, 30 assorted rockfish, 32 snapper, 34 grouper, and an astounding 46 species of sharks. In some cases, both fresh and saltwater species share the same generic name, and a few groupings are even more confusing: e.g., eight species of eels versus nine species of morays, and 14 species of rays alongside another 14 species of stingrays. Records are even kept for 29 species better known as baitfish: 17 different mackerel, seven mullet, three needlefish, and two herring. Three goldfish ornament the all-tackle list, including one of nine pounds.[3] Happily, there is only one record species for Japanese conger and another for madai, no doubt vindicating Mike Leech's fruitless search for mounted examples. A surprising number of the world's most popular game fish are also listed as solitary entries, including barramundi, bluegill, cobia, permit, swordfish, tarpon, wahoo, and walleye. Clearly, however, the IGFA's responsibility for keeping straight so many other like-named species has become increasingly complex.

---

[3]*Mike Leech was against adding goldfish (koi) but was overruled by Harry.*

An early tournament-winning tarpon taken by a young Erl Roman (right). Despite the continuing interest of anglers, remarkably little remains known about this species.

Originally, much discussion was given over to which fish were even deserving of world record status. Some species were obvious, but others much less so. As IGFA President Bill Carpenter noted in his correspondence, the underlying question — what constitutes a game fish? — was not easily answered. Carpenter's own answer — those most commonly sought by sportsmen — was clumsy and vague. Spearfish, two acrobatic but rarely encountered species of billfish, were at first considered too obscure for record consideration and not granted record status until the 1980s. Although most species of sharks are not known for their fighting qualities, many were listed as world record species simply due to their size and ubiquity. Nevertheless, with the exception of the valiant mako shark, IGFA founder Mike Lerner held most sharks in contempt, and early shark records were kept separately.[4,5]

---

[4]His justification was that sharks were cartilaginous fish and lacked the bony skeletons of other game species.
[5]In contrast, Zane Grey was an early shark enthusiast and rated the mako among the world's supreme game fish. He was also the subject of one of the greatest lines ever uttered in the annals of sport fishing. Once, when Grey witnessed an enormous shark alongside his vessel in the South Pacific, he was described at the moment as being, "not Zane Grey, but ashen grey."

World record certificate for Atlantic bluefin tuna caught by Kip Farrington in 1930. Note the 6-thread linen line class.

SPECIES	SCIENTIFIC NAME	WEIGHT	PLACE	DATE	ANGLER
Shark, blacktip reef	*Carcharhinus melanopterus*	13.55 kg 29 lb 13 oz	Coco Island Indian Ocean	Oct. 22, 1995	Dr. Joachim Kleidon
Shark, blue	*Prionace glauca*	239.49 kg 528 lb 0 oz	Montauk Point New York, USA	Aug. 9, 2001	Joe Seidel
Shark, bonnethead	*Sphyrna tiburo*	10.76 kg 23 lb 11 oz	Cumberland Sound Georgia, USA	Aug. 5, 1994	Chad Wood
Shark, bull	*Carcharhinus leucas*	316.50 kg 697 lb 12 oz	Malindi Kenya	Mar. 24, 2001	Ronald de Jager
Shark, Caribbean reef	*Carcharhinus perezi*	69.85 kg 154 lb 0 oz	Molasses Reef Florida, USA	Dec. 29, 1996	Rene G. de Dios
Shark, dusky	*Carcharhinus obscurus*	346.54 kg 764 lb 0 oz	Longboat Key Florida, USA	May 28, 1982	Warren Girle
Shark, Galapagos	*Carcharhinus galapagensis*	85.45 kg 188 lb 6 oz	Midway Islands Pacific Ocean	Aug. 15, 2000	David B. Holmer
Shark, great hammerhead	*Sphyrna mokarran*	449.51 kg 991 lb 0 oz	Sarasota Florida, USA	May 30, 1982	Allen Ogle
Shark, Greenland	*Somniosus microcephalus*	775.00 kg 1708 lb 9 oz	Trondheimsfjord Norway	Oct. 18, 1987	Terje Nordtvedt
Shark, gulper	*Centrophorus uyato*	7.34 kg 16 lb 3 oz	Bimini Bahamas	July 15, 1997	Doug Olander
Shark, gummy	*Mustelus antarcticus*	30.80 kg 67 lb 14 oz	Mcloughins Beach Victoria, Australia	Nov. 15, 1992	Neale Blunden
Shark, lemon	*Negaprion brevirostris*	183.70 kg 405 lb 0 oz	Buxton North Carolina, USA	Nov. 23, 1988	Colleen D. Harlow
Shark, leopard	*Triakas semifasciata*	18.42 kg 40 lb 10 oz	Oceanside California, USA	May 13, 1994	Fred Oakley
Shark, milk	*Rhizoprionodon acutus*	5.00 kg 11 lb 0 oz	Archipelago dos Bijagos Guinea Bissau	Apr. 1, 2001	Adrien Bernard
Shark, narrowtooth	*Carcharhinus brachyurus*	242.00 kg 533 lb 8 oz	Cape Karikari New Zealand	Jan. 9, 1993	Gaye Harrison-Armstrong
Shark, night	*Carcharhinus signatus*	76.65 kg 169 lb 0 oz	Bimini Bahamas	July 13, 1997	Ron Schatman
Shark, nurse	*Ginglymostoma cirratum*	109.58 kg 241 lb 9 oz	South Beach, Ft. Pierce Florida, USA	Apr. 14, 2001	Jeffery L. Chism
Shark, oceanic whitetip	*Carcharhinus longimanus*	167.37 kg 369 lb 0 oz	San Salvador Bahamas	Jan. 24, 1998	Reid Hodges
Shark, pig-eye	*Carcharhinus amboinensis*	45.50 kg 100 lb 4 oz	Moreton Bay Australia	Mar. 29, 2003	Gordon Macdonald
Shark, porbeagle	*Lamna nasus*	230.00 kg 507 lb 0 oz	Pentland Firth Caithness, Scotland	Mar. 9, 1993	Christopher Bennett
Shark, salmon	*Lamna ditropis*	104.32 kg 230 lb 0 oz	Port Gravina Alaska, USA	June 13, 2002	Ken Higginbotham
Shark, sand tiger	*Odontaspis taurus*	158.81 kg 350 lb 2 oz	Charleston Jetty South Carolina, USA	Apr. 29, 1993	Mark Thawley
Shark, sandbar	*Carcharhinus plumbeus*	240.00 kg 529 lb 1 oz	Archipelago des Bijagos Guinea Bissau	Apr. 5, 2002	Patrick Sebile
Shark, scalloped hammerhead	*Sphyrna lewini*	152.40 kg 335 lb 15 oz	Latham Island Tanzania	Dec. 3, 1995	Jack Reece, Q.P.M.
Shark, sevengill	*Notorynchus cepedianus*	32.80 kg 72 lb 4 oz	Weymouth Channel Manukou Harbour, New Zealand	Oct. 23, 1995	Shane Sowerby
Shark, shortfin mako	*Isurus oxyrinchus*	553.84 kg 1221 lb 0 oz	Chatham Massachusetts, USA	July 21, 2001	Luke Sweeney
Shark, sicklefin lemon	*Negaprion acutidens*	10.60 kg 23 lb 5 oz	Darwin Harbour Australia	Dec. 7, 1998	Craig Johnston
Shark, silky	*Carcharhinus falciformis*	346.00 kg 762 lb 12 oz	Port Stephen's N.S.W., Australia	Feb. 26, 1994	Bryce Robert Henderson
Shark, silvertip	*Carcharhinus albimarginatus*	180.60 kg 398 lb 2 oz	Malindi Kenya	Sept. 16, 2001	Billy Furnish
Shark, sixgilled	*Hexanchus griseus*	588.76 kg 1298 lb 0 oz	Ascension Island Atlantic Ocean	Nov. 21, 2002	Clemens Rump
Shark, smallfin gulper	*Centrophorus moluccensis*	2.40 kg 5 lb 4 oz	Lae, Huon Gulf Papua New Guinea	Feb. 13, 1993	Justin Mallett
Shark, smooth hammerhead	*Sphyrna zygaena*	164.65 kg 363 lb 0 oz	Horta Faial, Azores	July 31, 1999	Georg Geyer
Shark, spinner	*Carcharhinus brevipinna*	89.70 kg 197 lb 12 oz	Malindi Kenya, East Africa	Sept. 21, 1999	Emiel Van De Werf
Shark, thresher	*Alopias vulpinus*	348.00 kg 767 lb 3 oz	Bay of Islands New Zealand	Feb. 26, 1983	D.L. Hannah
Shark, tiger	*Galeocerdo cuvier*	807.40 kg 1780 lb 0 oz	Cherry Grove South Carolina, USA	June 14, 1964	Walter Maxwell
Shark, tope	*Galeorhinus galeus*	33.00 kg 72 lb 12 oz	Parengarenga Harbor New Zealand	Dec. 19, 1986	Melanie B. Feldman
Shark, velvet belly lantern	*Etmopterus spinax*	0.85 kg 1 lb 13 oz	Langesundbukta Norway	Oct. 7, 2000	Arild Borresen
Shark, white	*Carcharodon*	1208.38 kg	Ceduna South Australia	Apr. 21, 1959	Alfred Dean

The IGFA maintains all-tackle records for some 46 different species of sharks.

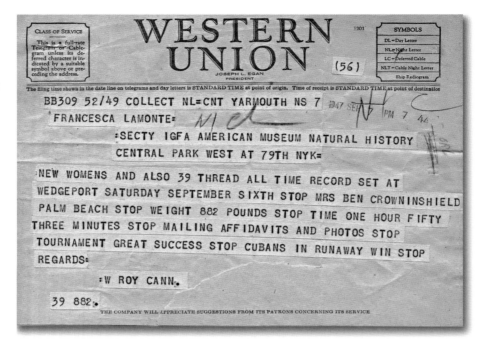

Post-war telegram from W. Roy Cann to Francesca LaMonte notifying her of another record-breaking tuna catch off Nova Scotia.

WESTERN UNION

CLASS OF SERVICE
This is a full-rate Telegram or Cablegram unless its deferred character is indicated by a suitable symbol above or preceding the address.

1201

SYMBOLS
DL = Day Letter
NL = Night Letter
LC = Deferred Cable
NLT = Cable Night Letter
Ship Radiogram

(56)

JOSEPH L. EGAN
PRESIDENT

The filing time shown in the date line on telegrams and day letters is STANDARD TIME at point of origin. Time of receipt is STANDARD TIME at point of destination

BB309 52/49 COLLECT NL=CNT YARMOUTH NS 7 1947 SEP PM 7 44

FRANCESCA LAMONTE=

=SECTY IGFA AMERICAN MUSEUM NATURAL HISTORY

CENTRAL PARK WEST AT 79TH NYK=

NEW WOMENS AND ALSO 39 THREAD ALL TIME RECORD SET AT
WEDGEPORT SATURDAY SEPTEMBER SIXTH STOP MRS BEN CROWNINSHIELD
PALM BEACH STOP WEIGHT 882 POUNDS STOP TIME ONE HOUR FIFTY
THREE MINUTES STOP MAILING AFFIDAVITS AND PHOTOS STOP
TOURNAMENT GREAT SUCCESS STOP CUBANS IN RUNAWAY WIN STOP
REGARDS=

=W ROY CANN.

39 882.

THE COMPANY WILL APPRECIATE SUGGESTIONS FROM ITS PATRONS CONCERNING ITS SERVICE

As recreational angling grew in the post-war years, the proliferation of small boats and new recreational fishing opportunities inshore served to make sport fish out of many less sizable species. Gradually, smaller but more popular game fish were added to the record-keeping rolls, including bonito, grouper, kawakawa, and snapper. A few species were added but later dropped for lack of interest,[6] and several closely-related weakfish were so difficult to tell apart that a single record entry covered all weakfish species until 1997. Twenty years before, the IGFA had already begun to witness growing criticism of its drift away from big-game fishing, but the recreational market was changing and the organization was anxious to broaden its appeal. Illustrating the swing, a subsequent internal study of all record submissions over a recent five-year period[7] showed a median weight of just 7 lb for freshwater and 12 lb for saltwater species, bearing out the IGFA's contention that recreational angling today is a lot more than just big-game fishing.

Nevertheless, the setting of early big-game records was given enormous play, especially during the war years when distractions were of premium value. When Mr. K.L. Ames caught a 133 lb wahoo in the Bahamas in April of 1943, the *Miami Herald* ran a front-page story on the accomplishment and it was subsequently carried by the Associated Press wire around the world. The coverage included mention of many Florida pioneers: Miami Rod &

[6] *e.g., sawfish and hammerhead shark, both later reinstated.*
[7] *From 1999-2003.*

Reel Club secretary Don McCarthy, legendary angler and taxidermist Al Pflueger, and *Miami Herald* columnist Erl Roman. Ten years before, Roman had become a virtual one-man clearinghouse for world record claims as ever-larger tuna, sailfish, and marlin were pulled from nearby waters. Telegrams were often sent to Roman notifying him of more distant catches, and his weekly fishing columns were filled with new records, broken tackle, and high society. As it happened, his forwarding of all such correspondence and affidavits to Tommy Aitken at *Outdoor Life* created a record-keeping flap that actually helped hasten the founding of the IGFA.

Al Pflueger, champion angler and well-known Florida taxidermist.

Tommy Aitken (ca. 1938).

As noted earlier, the first listing of world record catches was published in 1921 by Van Campen Heilner in *Field & Stream* magazine. However, *Outdoor Life* Fishing Editor Tommy Aitken began publishing his own record listing in 1935 with details drawn partly from Roman and partly from consultations with Heilner's co-compiler Francesca LaMonte at the American Museum of Natural History. When Aitken's first world record chart appeared, a minor scandal erupted in that no credit had been given either to the Museum or *F&S*. The Museum wrote *Outdoor Life* asking for a credit line, and Aitken responded with an excited multi-page letter noting the extent to which many of the *OL* records came from his own files. Finally, after much typewriter ink was expended, the flap was resolved when *OL* agreed to give both the Museum and *F&S* credit in future printings. If nothing else, the need for a single clearinghouse for record-keeping had become abundantly clear.

206

Aitken's publication of his own record listings in Outdoor Life *spawned a minor controversy and emphasized the need for a single record-keeping entity.*

GAME-FISH RECORDS
Compiled by THOMAS AITKEN

MAJOR WORLD'S RECORDS*

* Confusion of species, the use of different names in various parts of the world, and failure of anglers to file complete data leave many records open. These include white and silver marlin, dolphin, the various bonito species, and false albacore.

† The white shark is recognized as a game fish for the first time, since it is as well qualified for the classification as the mako shark.

‡ Guild tuna, also recognized for the first time, was identified by Henry W. Fowler, Academy of Natural Sciences, Philadelphia, as a new species (Semathunnus guildi), and was first caught in 1933 off Tahiti by Eastham Guild.

SPECIES	LBS.	YEAR	ANGLER	WHERE CAUGHT
ALBACORE	66¼	1912	Frank Kelly	Catalina, Cal.
AMBERJACK	95	1916	S. W. Eccles	Long Key, Fla.
BASS (channel)	74	1929	Chas. D. Beckmann	Chincoteague, Va.
BASS (striped)	73	1913	Chas. B. Church	Vineyard Sound, Mass.
KINGFISH (king mackerel)	73½	1935	Lerner B. Harrison	Off Bimini, B. W. I.
MARLIN (black)	976	1926	Laurie D. Mitchell	Bay of Islands, N. Z.
MARLIN (blue)	636	1935	Thomas H. Shevlin	Off Bimini, B. W. I.
MARLIN (striped)	692	1931	Alfonse Hamann	Off Balboa, Cal.
SAILFISH (Atlantic)	106	1929	W. A. Bonnell	Off Miami Beach, Fla.
SAILFISH (Pacific)	180	1931	William B. Gray	Gulf of Panama.
SHARK (mako)	798	1931	H. White-Wickham	Bay of Islands, N. Z.
SHARK (white)†	998	1935	Francis H. Low	Off N. J. Coast.
SWORDFISH (broadbill)	837½	1934	W. E. S. Tuker	Off Tocopilla, Chili.
TARPON	242½	1934	Jax M. Cowden	Panuco River, Mex.
TUNA (Allison)	216	1934	C. M. Cooke III	Off Hawaii
TUNA (Guild)‡	176	1933	Aksel Wichfeld	Off Tahiti
TUNA (blue-fin)	851	1933	L. Mitchell-Henry	Off Whitby, Eng.
WAHOO	124¾	1935	J. B. Stickney	Off Hawaii
YELLOWTAIL	111	1926	Zane Grey	Bay of Islands, N. Z.

U. S. COASTAL RECORDS
(Other than those included in above chart)

SPECIES	LBS.	YEAR	ANGLER	WHERE CAUGHT
MARLIN (blue)	247	1935	Russell Stoddard, Jr.	Off Miami Beach, Fla.
TUNA (blue-fin)	705	1933	Francis H. Low	Off New York Harbor.
TUNA (Allison)	132	1934	Thomas Snyder	Off Long Key, Fla.
TARPON	213	1901	N. M. George	Bahia Honda, Fla.
WAHOO	78	1929	T. D. M. Cordeza	Key West, Fla.

NORTH AMERICAN RECORDS*
(Other than those included in the World's Records)

* Conflicting reports from Nova Scotia tend to confuse the North American tuna records. Until more definite data are submitted these will be considered open.

SPECIES	LBS.	YEAR	ANGLER	WHERE CAUGHT
BASS (white sea)	60	1904	C. H. Harding	Off Catalina, Cal.
BLUEFISH	25	1874	L. Hathaway	Cohasset, Mass.
BONEFISH	13¾	1919	B. F. Peek	Off Bimini, B. W. I.
SHARK (mako)	786	1935	Ernest Hemingway	Off Bimini, B. W. I.
SWORDFISH (broadbill)	573	1927	George C. Thomas III	Off Catalina, Cal.
WEAKFISH	17-3/16	1933	F. J. Conzen	Peconic Bay, N. Y.
WAHOO	86	1911	W. E. Carlin	Off New Providence, B. W. I.

WORLD'S RECORDS by WOMEN
(Major records only)

SPECIES	LBS.	YEAR	ANGLER	WHERE CAUGHT
AMBERJACK	86	1935	Mrs. W. H. Kirn	Off Bimini, B. W. I.
KINGFISH (king mackerel)	58	1927	Miss Mae Haines	Off Long Key, Fla.
MARLIN (black)	823	1932	Mrs. Eastham Guild (Carrie Fin)	Off Cape Brett, N. Z.
MARLIN (striped)	402	1934	Mrs. Carl W. Carson	Off Catalina, Cal.
MARLIN (blue)	326	1935	Mrs. Michael Lerner	Off Bimini, B. W. I.
SAILFISH (Atlantic)	71	1928	Mrs. John T. Dorrance	Off Long Key, Fla.
SAILFISH (Pacific)	165	1931	Miss Peggy Hardwick	Off Cocos Island, Costa Rica.
SWORDFISH (broadbill)	426	1921	Mrs. Keith Spalding	Off Catalina, Cal.
SWORDFISH (Atlantic)	245	1931	Mrs. Oliver Grinnell	Off Montauk, N. Y.
TUNA (blue-fin)	175	1935	Mrs. S. Kip Farrington, Jr.	Off Wedgeport, N. S.
TUNA (Allison)	123½	1935	Mrs. O. L. Schubert	Off Miami Beach, Fla.
TARPON	210	1915	Mrs. W. Ashby Jones	Caloosahatchee River, Fla.

Copyright, 1936
OUTDOOR LIFE
Corrected to Jan. 1, 1936

A mutilated fish is never accepted as a record. Weighing of fish must be witnessed. Fish must be caught on rod and reel in an ethical, "legal," and sportsmanlike manner. Observance of tackle specifications and accepted angling-club rules prevailing in the locality where fish was caught usually make it eligible for recognition.

Reprinted from the February 1936 Issue Outdoor Life

Interestingly, while the two sets of records agreed on most entries, *Outdoor Life* appeared to hold to a somewhat higher standard. In 1934, a 119 lb Atlantic sailfish caught jointly by Ernest Hemingway and J.S. McGrath was accorded world record status by *F&S* but was disallowed by *Outdoor Life* which continued to honor a smaller 106 lb fish taken in 1929 by a single angler. It may have been that Aitken hoped that his own records would serve as the foundation for IGFA's record-keeping, but *Field & Stream's* association with the Museum was hard to overlook. Nevertheless, Aitken's public and private support for a governing body for big-game angling contributed mightily to the IGFA's founding, and he was a friend to the organization until his death. Probably as a result of not being a world-class fisherman himself, Aitken was never properly given his due.

Despite this slight, Aitken's fussiness did enormous credit to the accuracy of early IGFA records. In lengthy letters to Lerner that still survive today, Aitken went to painstaking and no doubt satisfying lengths in pointing out the sloppiness of *Field & Stream's* original record-keeping. In one missive, Aitken noted that the striped marlin record awarded to Alphonse Hamann incorrectly identified the fish as being taken off Balboa City, Panama Canal Zone when it was actually captured off Balboa, California. In that Francesca LaMonte had been originally charged by Lerner with vetting the records inherited from *Field & Stream*, Aitken and LaMonte were frequently at odds.[8] Nevertheless, the rigor that both parties brought to the record verification process generated a culture of exactitude that continues to exist to this day.

---

[8]*Indeed, in a private note to Lerner, she saw Aitken as wanting her job.*

Before the Lerner Expeditions began in 1936, the AMNH relied largely on anglers for information concerning pelagic game fish. This 1931 letter to Zane Grey from Francesca LaMonte apparently accepting Grey's pronouncement of a new species of marlin reflects the uncertainty of the day.

IN RE   CABLE ADDRESS "MUSEOLOGY NEW YORK"

THE AMERICAN MUSEUM OF NATURAL HISTORY

77TH STREET AND CENTRAL PARK WEST
NEW YORK CITY

DEPARTMENT OF ICHTHYOLOGY
FOUNDED BY BASHFORD DEAN
WILLIAM K. GREGORY, Ph.D., CURATOR
JOHN T. NICHOLS, A.B., CURATOR OF RECENT FISHES
E. W. GUDGER, Ph.D., BIBLIOGRAPHER AND ASSOCIATE
FRANCESCA R. LA MONTE, A.B., ASSISTANT CURATOR

CHARLES H. TOWNSEND, Sc.D., RESEARCH ASSOCIATE
C. M. BREDER, JR., RESEARCH ASSOCIATE
LOUIS HUSSAKOF, Ph.D.,
    RESEARCH ASSOCIATE IN DEVONIAN FISHES
VAN CAMPEN HEILNER, M.Sc., FIELD REPRESENTATIVE

8 July, 1931.

Dear Dr. Grey:

May we have your permission to reproduce the photograph you sent us of yourself standing beside the Giant Tahitian Striped Marlin (1040 lbs.), as the heading for the section on Gamefishes in our forthcoming Guide to the Fish Collections in the American Museum of Natural History?

Sincerely,

Francesca LaMonte

Francesca LaMonte

Dear Miss LaMonte

Delighted to oblige you. I will send you photos of world record Sailfish and 810 pd Black marlin for your file.

Yours hastily

Z. G.

Today the world record certification process takes place at IGFA headquarters and resembles a well-oiled machine. All applications must be submitted within 60 days of capture if made within the U.S., or 90 days if made abroad. In addition to the completed application form, all entries must include a line or tippet sample, assorted photographs, proof of scale certification, a signed and notarized affidavit, and the required fee.[9] A list of witnesses is highly desirable but not required. Likewise, narration and videotapes that add detail are helpful but not vital inclusions. Exacting requirements for submissions in all categories are listed in the *WRGF* annual and various other IGFA publications. If the list seems unnecessarily onerous, it is rightly designed to eliminate as much subjectivity from the approval

_____

[9]*Requirements vary slightly for fly applications and are somewhat less exacting for juniors.*

process as possible. Given the fact that many hundreds of new records are approved each year, most anglers seem able to successfully navigate the procedures.

Upon receipt in Florida, the application package is logged in by the world record administrator, checked for glaring omissions, entered into the IGFA's database, and the required line[10] sample tested for breaking strength. Prior to testing, the line is stored for seven days in controlled conditions to stabilize its breaking strength, then soaked for two hours in fresh water before being stressed.[11] Five separate tests are performed by a highly-sophisticated $35,000 machine, the results of which are averaged to determine a final rating.[12] Prior to 1949, line testing was unnecessary because lines were rated by thread count and not breaking strength. However, manufacturing tolerances improved thereafter with the development of synthetic lines, and today some makers use line class as a guarantee of minimum rather than maximum breaking strength. As a result, line over-testing is the most common reason for record denial, and overcoming this hurdle at the beginning of the process eliminates much needless work later on.

---

[10]*Or tippet.*
[11]*Note that line cannot be pre-tested in lieu of testing after the catch is made.*
[12]*Line strength can now be calculated to 1/100th of a pound.*

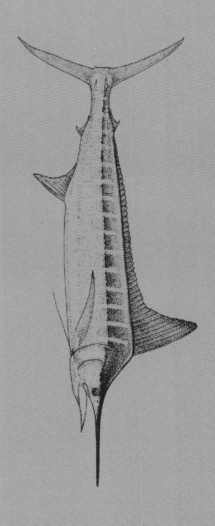

While occasionally incorrect, Grey was rarely timid in making claims of discovery.

This IGFA world record certificate to Chisie Farrington in 1949 was among the first granted on the basis of line class breaking strength and not thread count.

If all preliminary requirements have been met, the application is then cloaked in a distinctive white jacket and forwarded to the IGFA's resident biologist. That office is responsible for using the appropriate length/girth formula[13] to estimate weight and making sure that figure is not in conflict with the scale weight. Photographs are then checked to confirm proper species identification, and the scientific name of the catch is appended to the file. Any other matters of ichthyological interest or concern are also noted,[14] and the package is reviewed for rules violations. If the biologist has any questions or concerns, he/she may contact the applicant for more details. If all requirements have been met, the jacketed application is then forwarded to the IGFA's senior staff and President for final review and approval. Thereafter, the package is returned to the records administrator and the claimant notified of the IGFA's ruling.

Generally the entire approval process takes about 90 days and is intentionally slow to allow all information to accumulate. Historically, some 25-40% of all record applications are ultimately rejected, most due to line over-testing or the presence of a larger previously-approved but as-yet unpublished record. Not infrequently, potential saltwater records are disqualified due to a longer-than-allowed leader and/or double line, and

---

[13]*Depending on species; for billfish, the calculation is generally (girth x girth x length) divided by 800.*

[14]*For example, unusual distribution or size. Such information is passed onto affinity groups and scientific organizations, resulting in the IGFA's frequent citing as a primary source in research papers.*

the IGFA does not permit exceptions for even the smallest overage. One recent application for a woman's blue marlin record was rejected when the combined length of the leader and double line measured 1" too long. To its further credit, the IGFA is always willing to reexamine its record decisions if given proper cause. In 1973, the IGFA retired the men's 12-lb line class record for Pacific blue marlin when new photographs indicated that the fish was actually a black marlin. On another occasion, pictures of a record-setting 51 lb permit created an uproar when local fishermen protested that the fish in the photographs couldn't possibly have weighed that much. Further investigation failed to provide definitive proof, and the record was rescinded.

Alfred Dean's 2,664 lb white shark taken in Australia in 1959, the largest IGFA all-tackle record of any species.

Although the IGFA now allows for co-record holders, a 1945 dispute between two similarly-sized weakfish resulted in a decision to require a minimum margin for new record consideration. In that case, the marginally-larger fish[15] was awarded the undisputed title, but the IGFA thereafter required a four-ounce margin to reduce fractional record submissions and account for the vagaries in scale accuracy. In 1952, the required differential changed to one pound for records of 100 lb or more and one-half pound for records under that weight. Later, the addition of many smaller record species caused further adjustments, and currently the required overage is two ounces on records under 25 lb and .005% on anything larger. All record submissions must be in excess of one pound, thereby dashing the hopes of some 20,000 tiny finned species of ever achieving world record status.

Of the nearly 1,000 all-tackle world records currently on the IGFA's books, various circumstances strongly suggest that some will never be broken. The fishery for California black sea bass has been closed for many years, ensuring the existing record holders' status for the foreseeable future. Likewise, great white sharks are protected in Australia, South Africa and the U.S., where they most often occur. In addition, many of the massive shark records were probably set with the help of mammal chum in shallow water, a practice banned under current rules. The two largest bonefish on record were taken in Zululand in a manner almost certainly not akin to that of bonefishing in the Bahamas, and most biologists suspect the presence of a second bonefish species in that region. Other records for alligator gar, Pacific sailfish, and swordfish have stood for more than 50 years and are unlikely to be broken anytime soon.

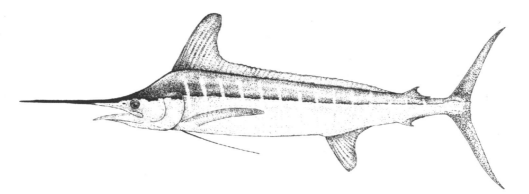

Several records of long standing also make for good stories. A 122 lb white marlin taken off Bimini in 1953 by a junior college student has remained the women's 12-lb world record for more than 50 years, despite the angler's complete inexperience in the sport. Her world record file includes a charming period photograph of the joyously-smiling young angler amidst a lush tropical setting. In 1982, a virtually unbreakable women's

[15]*By three ounces.*

world record was set by Kay Mulholland with her capture of a 998 lb black
marlin on 20-lb test line. Her application indicated that the fish was brought
to gaff in only three minutes, prompting an inquiry as to how she was able
to accomplish that feat. Her lengthy response was more than satisfactory and
concluded by stating she had been trying to set the record for seven years:
thus, the true time of capture was really seven years plus three minutes.

Remarkable all-tackle records of note include Ken Fraser's capture in 1979
of an unimaginably-huge 1,496 lb Atlantic bluefin tuna off Nova Scotia.
Thoroughly documented to the IGFA's satisfaction, no tuna captured since
that time has even approached Fraser's mark. Elsewhere, Abe Sackheim's
capture in 1960 of an enormous 114 lb roosterfish in La Paz, Mexico was
the event of a lifetime for this elderly San Diego angler. Taken on light
tackle in just 20 minutes, the fish surpassed the previous world record by an
astonishing 38 lb. Joey Pallotta's 468 lb white sturgeon caught off Bernicia,
California in 1983 took five hours to land and remains the largest freshwater
fish in the annals of IGFA record-keeping. One year earlier, Albert
McReynolds hit paydirt with his capture of an all-tackle record
78 lb striped bass. The lucky angler was paid $250,000 for his record catch
by a tackle company, underlining the enormous modern-day stakes in world
record accreditation.

IGFA files also include many engaging examples of rejected records. When in 1941 a record submission was received by Ned Schafer for a 780 lb tuna taken on 24-thread line, it was subsequently disqualified for having been shot into submission. However, at about the same time, a properly-captured 880 lb tuna was caught by professional boatman Jack Carpenter and was subsequently awarded world record status. Schafer was incensed and lodged a formal complaint with the IGFA's Executive Committee. Upon reviewing the circumstances of both catches, Ernest Hemingway was prompted to write that Schafer was both "unsportsmanlike and crybabyish" (sic), and the world-famous author pronounced himself fully prepared to heap public ridicule on poor Mr. Schafer should the latter persist with his claim. With that, the matter was settled.

Hemingway was also involved in a controversy surrounding the capture of a record-breaking silver marlin[16] off Hawaii during the 1940s. The angler utilized a new hinged fighting chair that had just been introduced, and the record catch prompted Hemingway to inspect the heretofore unfamiliar device. In a handwritten letter to Lerner, he promptly decried the great advantage that such a mechanism provided to the angler. While visiting Hawaii shortly thereafter, the IGFA's newly-appointed Field Representative Philip Wylie followed up on Hemingway's inspection and concurred with his assessment, pointing out the endless permutations that could arise once the concept had been approved in principle. In short order, the innovation was banned.

---

[16]Note previous discussions surrounding the non-existent silver marlin.

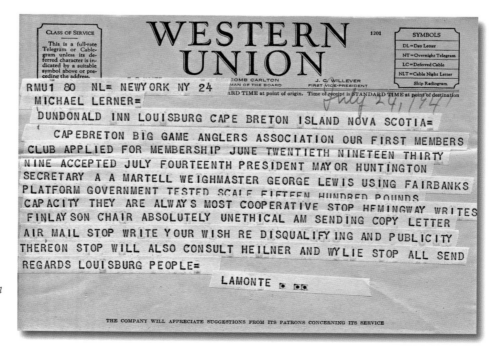

Among other news, this 1941 telegram from Francesca LaMonte to Mike Lerner left little doubt as to Ernest Hemingway's opinion on the new hinged fighting chair.

214

In 1957, an interesting record submission was received from George T. Bruns for his capture of an 8 lb 12 oz sand bass in California. The angler based his entry on the fact that the existing world record for Atlantic "sea bass" in the 20-lb line class was only 8 lb 3 oz. Moreover, the sand bass had been described in an official California Fish & Game publication as being identical to sea bass. Though ubiquitous in southern California, the sand bass was unknown to Francesca LaMonte and she admitted as much to the angler in a letter dated June 4, 1957. Nevertheless, his request for record recognition in the Atlantic sea bass category was denied, and the California sand bass remains unrecognized as a world record game fish to this day.

Lou Marron's capture of this 1,182 lb broadbill swordfish off Chile in 1953 clearly qualified as a trophy catch and remains the all-tackle record for this species.

Still other record submissions have prompted dramatic action. In 1968, George Hoag applied for record recognition as a result of his capture of a 23 lb 3 oz swordfish taken on 20-lb test line. After considerable discussion, his application was rejected on the premise that the catch was not substantial enough for the line class. Swordfish records in the surrounding line classes were much heavier,[17] and the capture of such a small fish had likely presented little challenge to the angler. Although consensus to deny the record claim was finally achieved, dissenters pointed out that records taken under similar circumstances were already in the books.[18] Ultimately, new wording was inserted in the world record requirements mandating that submissions must be considered "trophy sized,"[19] and maximum line classes were established for many smaller record species.

---

[17]*At the time, existing swordfish records for 12-lb and 30-lb line were 120 lb and 365 lb, respectively.*
[18]*e.g., a 31 lb bonito taken on 130-lb test line.*
[19]*Trophy-sized weight was loosely defined as being at least 50% of the all-tackle record weight.*

One-armed angler Louis Schmidt, Jr. (also with only one leg) and his 1,006 lb black marlin taken in Panama in 1949. This fish remains the first "grander" black marlin ever captured on rod and reel.

Record applications are routinely denied if the catch was not made in compliance with applicable law. One angler's recent submission of a blue marlin taken on 12-lb tippet was rejected because the fish was smaller than the 99" minimum size limit prescribed by the NMFS.[20] Although the catch was made off the Turks & Caicos Islands, it was captured by an American and thus subject to U.S. regulations. On another occasion, a potentially record-setting 33 lb snook was captured out of season, placed in a live well, weighed, and subsequently released. However, its presence in the live well was considered possession during a closed season, and the record claim was disallowed. Not infrequently, record-size bass are also submitted for consideration with trout as the indicated bait. In that the use of trout as bait is widely prohibited, these record submissions are likewise denied.

[20]*National Marine Fisheries Service, the governing American agency.*

Despite the rigidity of the record-granting process, the IGFA does have modest latitude. In a 1962 letter to the IGFA from Howard Carey, the angler regretfully acknowledged that his recent world record submission for a California black sea bass was invalid. On board a boat, Carey had fallen to the deck while fighting the giant fish, and his rod briefly came into contact with the boat's railing. He had forgotten the incident over the course of a three-hour fight, but it later came to mind after he had already submitted a world record application. Nevertheless, the IGFA's Executive Committee ruled that no substantive violation had occurred and reinstated his record claim.[21]

---

[21] *It also took the opportunity to commend him for his sportsmanship.*

Although no world record, this 1,805 lb Pacific blue marlin was the catch of a lifetime for Captain Cornelius Choy, his mate (and daughter) Gail, and their four passengers in 1970.

Occasionally, the IGFA has extended recognition to exceptional catches even when no record consideration is possible. In 1949, a record-weight black marlin was taken off Panama by Louis Schmidt Jr., a most remarkable sportsman with but one arm and one leg. After a nearly four-hour fight, Mr. Schmidt turned the rod over to his brother who captured the fish in another 35 minutes. While clearly ineligible for world record consideration,[22] the IGFA was pleased to award a well-earned certificate for Outstanding Achievement to the intrepid angler. Similar recognition was also conveyed to a British sportsman believed to be the only angler ever to capture three different species of shark over one thousand pounds. Nevertheless, noteworthy catches not taken in accordance with IGFA rules receive scant notice, including the capture of a 1,649 lb Atlantic blue marlin in 1984 and a 1,323 lb mako shark by two commercial fishermen in 1993. Now largely forgotten, both catches would have conveyed near-immortality to their successful anglers if taken with proper form.

---

[22]*Due to the participation of more than one angler.*

Texas big-game angler Alfred C. Glassell, Jr. and his 1,025 lb black marlin taken off Cabo Blanco, Peru in 1952. As Glassell noted in his letter to Lerner, this was "the first legal 1,000 lb game fish."

Perhaps the most remarkable story of an opportunity lost dates back to 1970 with the capture off Oahu, Hawaii of a breathtaking 1,805 lb Atlantic blue marlin. Adherence to IGFA regulations would have resulted in a virtually insurmountable all-tackle record for blue marlin and supplanted Alfred C. Glassell, Jr.'s 1,560 lb black marlin as the largest billfish ever taken in accordance with sporting rules. However, the hook was set by the captain and the fish was subsequently fought by four inexperienced anglers. What made the feat so remarkable was the presence of a fresh 150 lb yellowfin tuna in the marlin's gullet. As a result, the enormous fish was unable to do itself justice in the ensuing battle and was brought to gaff in only 45 minutes. The novice fishermen prevailed in record time, if not to record acclaim.

Over the years, the *International Angler* has been used as a vehicle to recognize singular events, such as the time in 1984 when twin sisters Gina and Toni Grimaldi caught identical 187 lb blue marlin on the same day and from the same boat while fishing off Bermuda. The vanquished have also been noted, as when angler Dennis Dunn lost a giant blue marlin off New Zealand after a 30-hour battle. Dunn was treated for blisters, sunburn and extreme fatigue at various times during the fight. After finally conceding defeat, the exhausted Dunn turned the rod over to the boat's crew whereupon the fish was finally lost after an additional two-hour tussle. Nevertheless, even that epic battle did not achieve the unofficial record for angling futility, as that dubious bit of immortality is still held by D.B. Heatley. In 1968, Heatley's struggle against a monster swordfish lasted an incredible 32 hours and five minutes before the fish made its escape.

Other angling events of startling novelty have also appeared in the *International Angler*. Among those are Barry Preston's capture in 1994 of a swordfish from the beach in Jervis Bay, Australia; Gil MacKinnon's hooking and landing a 163 lb bluefin tuna while surfcasting off Nauset Beach, Massachusetts in 1990; Dr. Alan Cordt's recapture of a striped bass he tagged one year earlier at the same location on Martha's Vineyard; IGFA Trustee Ruben Jaen's daytime capture in 1996 of five rod-and-reel swordfish in one day off Venezuela;[23] Captain Gary Choeste's "Boat Grand Slam" off

ALFRED C. GLASSELL, JR.
234 OIL & GAS BLDG.
HOUSTON, TEXAS

June 11, 1952

Dear Mike:

Since the beginning of time it has been the dream of man, particularly those who follow the Sea, to view or take a game fish weighing 1000 pounds.

On the fourth day of April, nineteen hundred and fifty two Mother Sea, for the first time, opened her arms and gave forth her first legal 1000 pound game fish. This fish was a Black Marlin taken in the waters off Cabo Blanco, Peru in the junction of the Humboldt and Ecuadorian currents and it was my great honor and privilege to be the happy angler.

Being aware of your keen interest in the Sea and fishing I feel sure you have followed this event with considerable interest.

It is with a great deal of pride and extreme joy that I am able to present you herewith a complimentary photograph of the greatest fish ever taken.

Sincerely yours,

Alfred

Mr. Michael Lerner
1112 DuPont Bldg.,
Miami, Florida

---

[23] *Made utilizing Jaen's newly-developed "deep drop" technique.*

Cocos Island[24] where a triple hook-up yielded one blue marlin, one striped marlin, and one sailfish; and Hank Manley's capture of five different billfish species[25] in one 24-hour period off Venezuela in 1997. Such events almost defy belief, but there they are.

Arguably the most famous record disqualification in the history of angling dates back to 1925. That was the year angler David Hayes landed a sizable smallmouth bass from Dale Hollow Lake, Tennessee. The fish was later weighed at the Cedar Hill Fish Camp and its weight recorded at 11 lb 15 oz. Hayes' record stood for 41 years despite being one of the most poorly substantiated marks in the *Field & Stream* files. Long believed to be unbeatable, no other smallmouth bass has ever been landed within one pound of his mark. When freshwater record-keeping responsibility was passed from *Field & Stream* to the IGFA in 1978, the Hayes file was inspected and doubts as to its validity resurfaced. Nevertheless, the record was duly certified...until freelance writer Eldon Davis stumbled across a startling affidavit in 1996. Apparently, Hayes' guide John Barlow had loaded the fish with 3 lb of lead sinkers prior to weigh-in but had undergone second thoughts about his misdeed some weeks after the fact. He subsequently signed a document with the US Army Corps of Engineers explaining the circumstances, but the affidavit was mislaid and forgotten until Davis came along. In short order, Hayes' fish was disqualified and the new record-holder became J.T. Gorman with his 10 lb 14 oz smallmouth taken at the same lake in 1969.[26]

That IGFA world records are still achievable is evidenced by the many hundreds of new records granted each year. Such records are set every day, and anyone fishing in accordance with IGFA rules has a chance at a record catch every time he or she wets a line. Unlike virtually any other sporting organization, the IGFA is unique in extending a world record opportunity to individuals in this way. To set a world record in pole vaulting or speed skating is beyond the hope of all but a few world-class athletes. In contrast, more than 500 new IGFA world records were granted to anglers of all kinds in 2004. Of those, some 130 were all-tackle records, indicating that many record-breaking catches are still there to be made. Successful applicants cross all demographic boundaries, giving the universe of IGFA world record-holders a unique diversity. A world record fish can come along any time, anyone might catch it, and that's what makes these stories of IGFA records and near-records so compelling. It could always happen to you.

---

[24]*Costa Rica.*

[25]*Blue marlin, white marlin, sailfish, long-billed spearfish, and swordfish.*

[26]*Controversy still swirls over this mark.*

10TO**1**CLUB
THE INTERNATIONAL GAME FISH ASSOCIATION
awards this certificate to

_____

for outstanding achievement in catchi...
weighing 10 times the wet test strength of t...

Species	Weight

Place of Catch	Date o...

In witness whereof, the undersigned have affixed...

President   Trust...

15TO**1**CLUB
THE INTERNATIONAL GAME FISH ASSOCIATION
awards this certificate to

_____

for outstanding achievement in catching a fish
weighing 15 times the wet test strength of the line used.

Weight

Date of Catch

In witness whereof, the undersigned have affixed their signatures.

Trustee

20TO**1**CLUB
THE INTERNATIONAL GAME FISH ASSOCIATION
awards this certificate to

_____

for outstanding achievement in catching a fish
weighing 20 times the wet test strength of the line used.

Species	Weight

Place of Catch	Date of Catch

In witness whereof, the undersigned have affixed their signatures.

President   Trustee

Although these popular award categories were discontinued in 1999, the IGFA still recognizes angling achievement in many ways.

The IGFA and other stewards of recreational angling must be increasingly vigilant to ensure future scenes like this one.

Chapter Eleven

A LOOK TO THE FUTURE

As the IGFA peers ahead into this third millennium, one thing is certain: recreational angling is bigger than ever. Recent surveys in Australia indicate that some 20% of the entire population regularly engage in fishing for pleasure. Their 3.36 million anglers spent nearly Au$2 billion on fishing equipment in 2001 and were foresighted enough to release one-third of all fish captured on rod and reel. In Europe, some 25 million people enjoy recreational angling at least one time per year, and their socioeconomic value to the European Union alone is estimated to exceed 25 billion euros per annum. Anglers in Europe and elsewhere are also becoming more political, lobbying aggressively for local and national legislation to protect their interests. The European Angling Alliance

---

[1] *Of this total, 80% describe themselves as saltwater anglers and 20% as freshwater enthusiasts, a proportion diametrically opposite to American anglers.*

was formed in 1994 and now represents 19 nations with more than five million affiliated anglers. As recreational angling continues to grow throughout the world, organized efforts to protect anglers' rights have arisen in dozens of different locales.

In the U.S., the story is little different. In 2001, more than 44 million Americans went fishing and directly spent some $41 billion in doing so. Estimates of indirect expenditures by American anglers range as high as $116 billion, dominating the entire sporting goods category in terms of economic impact. The jobs of nearly one million Americans relate directly or indirectly to recreational angling and generate some $30 billion in wages. Anglers abound in every state and territory, cross every demographic category, and include men and women from all walks of life. Indeed, one-third of anglers in America are women, making it one of the most popular outdoor pastimes among couples and families. Studies also indicate that youngsters who immerse themselves in fishing are less likely to fall prey to the temptations of crime and substance abuse during their formative years.

Before the advent of super-efficient seiners, capturing commercial quantities of tuna was often a hook-and-line proposition (photo courtesy NOAA).

Although not as voracious as the huge seiners, these fishermen use traps to capture giant tuna off Spain (photo courtesy NOAA).

In this and so many other ways does recreational angling add to the quality of life in America and beyond.

Nevertheless, arrayed against today's recreational angling interests are those of the commercial fishing industry, a divergence that has continued to widen over the years. The worldwide value of commercial landings is unquestionably enormous: the commercial sale of tuna alone generated $4 billion in 2002. One premium-grade tuna weighing 444 lb was recently auctioned at a Japanese fish market for an astonishing $173,600. In the United States, the National Marine Fisheries Service (NMFS) and its predecessor agencies have been collecting landing data since 1880 and conducting comprehensive regional surveys since 1951. In 2003, the NMFS estimated that commercial landings of finfish in the United States totaled 8.2 billion pounds with a dockside value of $1.5 billion. When shellfish are added into the mix, the total domestic numbers rise to 9.5 billion pounds and $3.4 billion. Worldwide figures are undoubtedly many times higher. Clearly, an industry of that size is capable of aggressive lobbying to protect its own interests and, in most matters of fisheries conservation, recreational and commercial interests are often diametrically opposed.

NOAA Fisheries with its National Marine Fisheries Service is the federal agency charged with protecting America's marine resources.

Unfortunately, the average recreational angler has little idea of how fisheries management actually works. Unlike the well-organized and well-funded commercial sector, the recreational angling community generally has not acquitted itself well in this critical arena. In particular, many big-game anglers have simply given up participating in conservation-related activities other than tag-and-release. Successes in the conservative management of most highly-migratory species have been rare and fleeting, and many offshore anglers are acutely conscious of the exclusive nature of their sport. Their high-minded arguments for conservation often wilt in the face of commercial fishermen struggling to support their families. Recreational anglers also find themselves squeezed between well-funded commercial interests and radical environmentalists. Where anglers might have served as a bridge of moderation between the two extremes, they have struggled to find their voice.

In the future, the IGFA's greatest challenge will be to cement its role as the voice of the world angling community. Its far-flung membership and roster of International Representatives are unique in providing on-the-water constituents in more than 130 countries. Other fisheries advocates tend to be more regional or species-specific in nature, allowing them more local focus but less global relevance. Indeed, the IGFA is the only recreational

Massive tuna seiners like this one take a huge toll.

angling advocate with a credible world view. However, all too many anglers today find the science surrounding fisheries management to be complex, the methodology stultifying, and the results arbitrary and indefinite. Largely as a result, international management of highly-migratory species such as tuna and billfish will continue to be a particularly difficult problem. Over-exploitation of most pelagic species will continue unless the world's offshore anglers can unite behind a single qualified and well-funded spokesman to overcome the influence of both commercial interests and environmental extremists. That the IGFA has not yet been able to achieve this unity is one of its greatest unfulfilled opportunities.

Nevertheless, there are some bright spots. Over the last 15 years, several regional inshore fisheries have enjoyed significant rebounds from points of near collapse, including redfish in the Gulf of Mexico, striped bass along the eastern seaboard, and halibut and white sea bass on the U.S. West Coast. Aggressive management and a rare unity of purpose among interested parties have been largely responsible, and certain other localized fisheries are showing similar signs of recovery. While management of pelagic species remains more difficult, the banning of longline fishing off Florida has resulted in a rebirth of the dormant recreational swordfishery there, and a similar ban along the west coast appears to have reversed a significant decline in local billfish stocks. Exciting new fisheries are also still emerging, including the discovery off Ghana in 1996 of enormous tuna and marlin.

To various degrees, the IGFA has participated in all of these events and is working to ensure that future successes will be equally significant.

As to its other major objectives, the IGFA has made remarkable progress. In particular, its angling rules and records continue to serve as category standards, its efforts on behalf of the recreational angler in both legislative and scientific matters are ever-increasing, and its Museum and Library remain unmatched. IGFA Trustees and Representatives participate in more than a thousand different activities relating to fisheries management worldwide, and current IGFA President Rob Kramer is committed to a conservation-oriented agenda that will further the global dialogue in this critical area. Internally, Kramer is working to streamline the IGFA's operations in order to focus on the organization's most promising programs and initiatives. Many matters remain in flux, but such is the nature of all long-lived things. However, there can be little doubt that modern-day anglers owe a profound debt of gratitude to Michael Lerner and his vision of an International Game Fish Association. Today's angling world is a far better place as a result of the IGFA's many sage years of stewardship.

228

These tuna shown here inside a seiner's net are now beyond the reach of recreational anglers.

THE INTERNATIONAL GAME FISH ASSOCIATION
TRUSTEE

THE INTERNATIONAL GAME FISH ASSOCIATION
OFFICER

Appendix A

IGFA LEADERSHIP

No international body that governs through voluntary compliance can survive for more than 65 years without extraordinary leadership. During that time, the following individuals have served critical roles as IGFA Executive Committee Members, Associates, Officers, and Trustees. Their contributions have been inestimable, and they are hereby saluted below.

INDEX